Congratulations
Cayden (or Bing)
on Your Baptism day.
Love,
Aunt Mary Jane and
Uncle Mike

BIBLE STORIES FOR GROWING KIDS

Bible

Stories
for GROWING KIDS

by Francine Rivers and Shannon Rivers Coibion

Illustrated by Pascale Constantin

Tyndale House Publishers, Inc. Carol Stream, Illinois

Visit Tyndale online at www.tyndale.com.

Check out the latest about Francine Rivers at www.francinerivers.com.

TYNDALE is a registered trademark of Tyndale House Publishers, Inc. The Tyndale Kids logo is a trademark of Tyndale House Publishers, Inc.

Bible Stories for Growing Kids

Designed by Jennifer Ghionzoli

Edited by Betty Free Swanberg

Library of Congress Cataloging-in-Publication Data

Rivers, Francine, date.

Bible Stories for Growing Kids / by Francine Rivers and Shannon Rivers Coibion.

  p.cm.

Includes index.

ISBN 978-1-4143-0569-1 (hc : alk. paper)

1. Bibles stories, English.   I. Coibion, Shannon Rivers.   II. Title.

BS551.3.R58 2007

220.9'505—dc22   2006017384

Printed in China

18 17 16 15 14 13

7 6 5 4 3 2

WITH LOVE TO

Brendan and Andrea Coibion
and William and Savannah Rivers

contents

New Testament

alphabetical list of Bible names

acknowledgments

My daughter, Shannon, and I want to give special thanks to our editor, Betty Swanberg. We had a vision to create a multigenerational book of stories and discussions about well-known and lesser-known Bible characters. However, Shannon (a homeschooling mom of two young children) and I (a writer of adult fiction) needed someone to come alongside us and teach us how to write this book. Betty has been that person, and we are grateful for the opportunity to work with her.

Thank you also to Karen Watson, who shared our vision, and to the Tyndale team for their combined efforts in placing this book in your hands.

Francine Rivers

A family adventure

We live in difficult times. Our children and grandchildren face issues and situations daily that challenge their faith, morality, and way of thinking. Teaching them *what* to think will not prepare them for the worldly philosophies they face. Teaching them *how* to think, reason, and apply God's truth to their own lives will better equip them to live in the world without becoming part of it. Therefore, it is with great excitement that Shannon and I, along with the Tyndale team, present this collection of stories and growing times to you and your family.

This is not intended to be just a children's book. We hope it will become a family adventure in which you share with one another truths from Scripture, life experiences, and the power of God to change lives. And what's most important of all is that you teach your children how to put God's teachings into practice every day.

I've written each fictionalized story from the point of view of one person. In some cases, several stories cover the same situation but from different perspectives. Once the story is read, Shannon's section, Growing Time, will help involve family members in open discussion about interesting historical facts. Then you'll find questions that go beyond facts and require deeper thinking about each individual and how the issues and challenges people faced thousands of years ago are those we still face today. The prayer suggestions will help teach the principle of praying through the truths from Scripture. Children are encouraged to pray that the lessons they learn will become evident in every part of their lives.

It is our prayer that this book will strengthen the faith of each family member and equip you to go into the world. As you learn from the lives of 30 of God's people, may you become better armed and ready to point the way by word and example to your Savior and Lord, Jesus Christ.

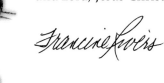

Francine Rivers

Dear reader,

Have you been listening to Bible stories and looking at Bible storybooks for as long as you can remember? Do you think you have learned everything there is to know about the people in the Bible? Well, guess what. I'm a mom, and I'm still learning! And guess what again. My mom is a grandmother, and she is still learning too!

The Bible is a very special book, because it is a gift from God. He wanted you, your parents, your grandparents, and everyone else to learn that He created people to be His friends. To help us understand that, He had many stories written down. Some of them are about people who learned to love and follow God. Others are about people who chose not to love or follow Him.

My mom, who is a good storywriter, thought it would be a good idea to learn as much as she could about 30 different Bible characters. She wanted to bring them to life through her writing. So she has written 30 stories about 30 Bible people for families just like yours. Her stories are in this book.

I'm a mom who homeschools my two children. We like to talk about Bible stories together as a family. We discover interesting facts about Bible times and talk about the people in the stories. We pray that we will learn the lessons they learned, and we ask God to help us not make the mistakes they made. I wrote the Growing Time pages in this book to help you and your family do the same.

We hope you will enjoy this book. But most of all, we pray that the stories and discussions will help you learn to be a better friend and follower of God and His Son, Jesus Christ.

With love from

Shannon Rivers Coibion

and from her mother

Francine Rivers

OLD TESTAMENT

Abram

Abram heard a voice. It came as a whisper, but he could feel the power of it. It was God who spoke!

"Leave your country and your relatives, and go to the land that I will show you. I will make you the father of a great nation. I will bless you with good things and make you famous. I will bless those who bless you and use bad things to curse those who curse you. But all the families of the earth will be blessed through you."

Abram went to his wife, Sarai. "We're leaving Haran and going wherever the Lord leads us."

Abram's nephew Lot came with them. They all packed their belongings, took their animals and servants, and traveled south. They camped beside an oak tree near the city of Shechem (SHE-kum) in the land of Canaan.

There the Lord appeared to Abram. "I am going to give this land to your children and their children."

Children! Abram and Sarai had no children, so God's

promise gave Abram hope. He built an altar for worshipping
God and called it Bethel, "the house of God."

After a while, a famine came to Canaan. No crops would
grow. Abram was so worried about providing food for his family
that he moved to Egypt without asking God what to do.

The Egyptian king, Pharaoh, wanted Sarai for himself.
Afraid for his life, Abram told the king that Sarai was his sister.
God was angry. When Pharaoh learned who Sarai was, he sent
her back to Abram.

Abram and Sarai left Egypt and took with them a maid
named Hagar to help Sarai.

When Abram and Sarai and Lot and all their servants
reached Canaan, they had so many animals there was not

enough water or grass to feed them all. Abram's servants began to fight with Lot's servants. Abram and Lot decided they must separate. Though Abram was older and deserved first choice, he asked Lot where he wanted to go. Lot chose the best piece of land. Abram stayed in Canaan.

After Lot went away, the Lord spoke to Abram again. "I am giving all this land to you and your children forever. I will give you so many people in your family that no one will be able to count them all!"

Years passed. Abram and Sarai grew old. Sarai gave up hope in God's promise of children. She told Abram to sleep with her servant, Hagar, and have a son. Abram did what Sarai asked, and Hagar gave birth to Ishmael (ISH-may-el).

When Abram was 99 years old and Sarai was almost 90, God changed Abram's name to Abraham. God also changed Sarai's name to Sarah. Then God visited them with two angels and told Abraham that Sarah would have a son within a year. Abraham believed, but Sarah laughed silently. So God told them their son's name would be Isaac, which means "laughter." And so it was, for they laughed with joy when their son was born.

One day Sarah saw Ishmael making fun of little Isaac, and Sarah feared for her son. She went to Abraham and told him to send Ishmael and Hagar away. The Lord told Abraham to listen to Sarah. Isaac was the child God had promised Abraham, and through Isaac blessings would come to the world.

Isaac grew up to be a fine boy. Abraham and Sarah loved him very much. God tested Abraham's faith by telling him to take Isaac to the top of a mountain and give him as an offering to God. So Abraham got up early in the morning, chopped wood, made bundles of food and coals, saddled his donkey, and set out for Mount Moriah (moh-RYE-uh) with Isaac.

As they walked up the mountain, Isaac said, "We have wood and fire, Father. But where is the lamb for the offering?"

"God will provide a lamb, Son." Abraham believed God would keep His promise of many children through Isaac. If he had to give up his son as an offering, Abraham trusted God to bring Isaac back to life.

When they reached the top of the mountain, Abraham placed the wood on a flat rock and put Isaac on the altar.

As Abraham took out his knife, God told him, "You can lay down the knife, Abraham. For now I know that you truly trust Me. Because you were willing to give your son as an offering to Me, I will bless you. And all the nations of the world will be blessed because you obeyed Me."

Jesus, the Messiah, Savior and Lord of the world, came from Abraham's family many years later. Abraham is called the father of everyone who has faith in God.

Scriptures: Genesis 12–13; 15–18; 21–22; Hebrews 11:17-19

growing time

Interesting Facts

- Abraham means "father of nations." Sarah means "princess." Their grandson Jacob had many grandchildren of his own. Their families became part of many nations. So Abraham really did become the "father of nations"!

- If there is not enough rain to make crops grow, there will not be enough grain to make bread and other food. Then people die, and we say there is a famine. Famines were common in Bible times because there often was no rain.

Truths from God's Word

God is pleased when we believe what He says and obey Him as Abraham did. Sometimes God has us wait a long time for His promises to come true. He wants us to trust in Him as we wait. Trusting in God is believing that He will do what He says.

Thinking about Abraham

God called Abraham His friend and made him the father of all those who have faith in the one true God. When God said all nations would be blessed through Abraham's family, God was speaking of the Messiah, Jesus Christ, who would save the world from sin. Name some times when Abraham didn't understand everything God was asking him to do. Can you tell about some ways Abraham showed that he trusted God, even when he didn't understand everything?

Thinking about YOUR Life

What are some things that God is asking you to do, but you don't understand why? Which of God's promises to you seem like they will take a long time? How can you show that you trust God to do what He says, no matter how long it takes?

Praying for Help to Trust

1. Pray that God will help you trust Him.

2. Ask for faith to believe that God will always answer your prayers at the right time.

3. Pray that God will help you follow and obey Him, even when you don't understand where He is leading you.

Hagar

"You belong to Abraham now." Hagar heard those words as she stood in the hall of Pharaoh's palace in Egypt. She and some other Egyptian people were "gifts" to Abraham, along with sheep, cattle, and donkeys. The people would be his servants, so they would do his chores but would not be paid for their work.

Hagar cried as she left her country. She wanted to stay, but as a servant she had no choice where she went. Abraham gave her to his wife, Sarah, to serve as her personal maid.

When they arrived in Canaan, Hagar watched Abraham worship an unseen God. She found this very strange, because statues of gods stood everywhere in her country. How could Abraham worship a god he could not see? Abraham even said he could hear God speak!

Abraham's wife, Sarah, cried sometimes, just as Hagar did.

And Hagar knew why. Sarah could not have children. One day Sarah surprised Hagar by ordering her to go to Abraham and be like a wife to him. "But if you and my husband have a baby together, the child will be mine."

Hagar obeyed Sarah and soon learned she was going to have a baby. Then she refused to behave like a servant anymore. After all, she was going to have the master's child.

Sarah became furious. "We will see which of us Abraham loves more!" After Sarah talked to her husband, she began to beat Hagar. Any time Hagar didn't do her work quickly enough, Sarah beat her again. Finally Hagar could not take it anymore and ran away.

The Lord found her drinking water from a desert spring along the road back to Egypt. "Hagar, where are you going?"

Hagar had never heard God speak before. His voice was filled with great power but was also tender and kind.

"I am running away from my mistress."

"Return to Sarah and do what she says. I will give you more people in your family someday than you can count. You will soon give birth to a son. Name him Ishmael (ISH-may-el), for I have heard how sad you are." (The name means "God hears.")

Hagar learned that Ishmael would be wild like a donkey and would quarrel with his family. But her son would never be a servant!

Hagar went back, content with the way her son's life was going to be. She never expected that God was going to perform a miracle and make it possible for Sarah to have a baby too. Abraham was 100, and Sarah was 90 years old! Sarah laughed, and they named the baby Isaac—which means "laughter."

Abraham threw a party when Isaac was ready for solid food. Ishmael watched the two old people with the toddler. He laughed at Isaac and said, "I am Abraham's first son."

Ishmael's mother, Hagar, agreed with him. "You will always be Abraham's first son. Everything that is his will someday belong to you, not Isaac. The master's son will serve you!" Ishmael laughed again.

But the next morning Abraham gave Hagar and Ishmael some food and water. "Go away," he said with tears in his eyes.

"And never come back." Abraham knew that God would take care of his son Ishmael, but he also knew that God had special plans for his son Isaac.

Now all her hopes were gone, and Hagar cried harder than she had ever cried before. She and her son wandered in the wilderness until all the food and water were gone. Ishmael was so thirsty he cried until he fell asleep and couldn't wake up.

Hagar left her son under a bush and sat on a rock, sobbing out a prayer to God. "I don't want to watch the boy die!"

God spoke. "Hagar, do not be afraid. I have heard Ishmael's cries. Go to him and comfort him, for I will make sure that he and his children and their families grow into a great nation."

When Hagar opened her eyes, she saw a well! She quickly removed the cover, filled her jar with water, and went to her son to give him a drink.

God kept His promise. Ishmael grew up and became very good with a bow and arrows. He married an Egyptian girl and had 12 sons. Their families grew into 12 large tribes scattered throughout the land. And all of them were enemies of Abraham's son Isaac.

Scriptures: Genesis 12:14-20; 16:1-16; 21:6-21; 25:12-18

growing time

Interesting Facts

- Ishmael and Isaac never got along. Ishmael grew up on the Sinai Peninsula, and many Arabs in that part of Egypt and surrounding countries today are proud to say they are descendants of Ishmael. Many Jewish people in Israel are proud to say they are descendants of Isaac. People from their families in the Middle East are still at war today.

- Did you ever hear the word *surrogate*? A surrogate parent is a stand-in parent. When a married couple cannot have children, sometimes they choose another person to have a baby for them. Abraham and Sarah ordered Hagar to become a surrogate parent for the child they thought they couldn't have.

Truths from God's Word

Sometimes people find themselves in a bad situation without it being any fault of their own. God is pleased when people keep trusting Him during the hard times. He wants everyone to have faith that He will turn bad situations into good ones.

Thinking about Hagar

Hagar was a servant who carried Abraham's baby inside her for nine months, knowing that Sarah would take the child when he was born. How do you think Hagar felt about that? What were some of the bad things that happened to her? What bad things happened to her son, Ishmael? How did God take her bad situation and turn it into something good?

Thinking about YOUR Life

As you grow up, your parents, teachers, and other adults have the right to tell you what to do. God expects you to honor these people by obeying them. Sometimes, though, you will feel that you have not been treated well. You may think you are in a situation that is not fair. It is up to you to trust God during this time and obey anyway. Can you think of a time when you were in a bad spot and God turned the situation into something good? What was it? How did you feel after it was over?

Praying about the Hard Times

1. Ask God to help you trust Him, even when you are in a situation that makes you feel sad and lonely.

2. Pray that you will believe God can turn bad situations into good ones.

3. Thank God for some of the good things He has already done for you.

Lot's Wife

Lot's Wife loved living in the city. Life was so much easier than it had been when she and her husband lived in a tent, caring for sheep and cows. Now her husband had a house in town. His servants took care of the flocks of sheep and herds of cattle in the fields outside of town.

A respected leader of the city, Lot sat at the city gates to welcome merchants and give advice to the people. Even more wonderful, Lot and his wife had arranged a marriage for each of their two daughters. They would marry sons of wealthy families who lived in Sodom. Life could not be better!

One night Lot came home with two handsome strangers.

Lot's wife wondered who the men were, because there seemed to be something unusually powerful about them. She washed their feet in welcome and offered them food.

Before the strangers could rest, someone pounded on the door and shouted, "Where are the men who came to spend the night with you? Bring them out so we can do what we want with them." They laughed. "We will treat them as if they are our wives."

Lot's wife shrugged. The city was full of such evil men, but one just had to ignore them to enjoy the other pleasures city life offered. Lot stepped outside. "The men are guests in my house and are under my protection."

The men outside became wild. Someone hit Lot and shoved him aside to pound on the door again. The two guests changed appearance, and Lot's wife knew they were angels! They opened the door. Light flashed. Men screamed. The angels pulled Lot inside and bolted the door. "We're blind!" the men outside cried.

"Do you have any other relatives here in the city?" The angels looked angry. "Get them out of this place. The rotten smell of sin has reached the Lord, and He has sent us to destroy the city."

Lot's wife wrung her hands. "What about the young men who plan to marry our daughters?"

Lot went to find them. When he came back, he shook his head. "They laughed at me. They thought I was joking!"

Early the next morning the angels called out, "Hurry!" This time they would not accept no for an answer. "Take your wife and two daughters and get out of here now, or you will die when the city is destroyed."

Lot's wife clung to him. "We can't go. We can't leave all this behind."

God was kind. He had the angels grab Lot by the hand, and Lot's wife and their daughters as well. The angels rushed them outside the city. "Run for your lives! And don't look back!"

They ran as fire came down like rain from heaven.

"My home!" Lot's wife moaned. "All my beautiful clothes! I forgot my jewelry!"

Weeping, Lot's wife turned back. The strong smell of sulfur filled her lungs as fire burned up the city and turned it to black rubble.

It was the last thing Lot's wife saw before she died standing, her body turned into a pillar of salt.

Scriptures: Genesis 13:5-13; 19:1-26

growing time

Interesting Facts

- Salt was used as money hundreds of years before Jesus was born. The word *salary* comes from salt, which was sometimes used to pay soldiers.

- You need salt (but not too much) to survive. Salt can season your food and help your body cool itself. It can also melt snow and ice!

- There is a Mount Sodom near the Dead Sea in the country of Israel. It is made of salt. This may be the place where God sent fire to destroy the city of Sodom.

Truths from God's Word

God does not want His children to become evil or worldly. God wants us to be like Him instead. God gives us the strength to obey Him. He sends us the help we need to follow Him, just as He sent angels to Lot and his family. However, He will punish those who turn away from Him. We must be willing to accept God's help.

Thinking about Lot's Wife

Lot's wife had the chance to escape from a city full of evil people, and yet she didn't want to leave. She had friends and money there. She didn't have faith that God would give her new friends and everything else she needed when she and her family moved. She chose the city over God. What are some things she may have been thinking as she turned to look back at Sodom and Gomorrah? Why do you think God chose to turn her into salt and not stone or something else? (Hint: If salt was used as money, perhaps salt was more important to Lot's wife than God.)

Thinking about YOUR Life

There are often things that God wants us to give up. Sometimes it is really hard to walk away from these things, but we are much happier when we listen to God. Are there any things right now that God wants you to walk away from? What are they? If you choose to follow God, what do you think will happen?

Praying about Avoiding Evil

1. Pray that God will help you walk away from evil things.

2. Ask God to show you how to follow Him and not turn back.

3. Pray for faith to believe God will protect you and your family from evil.

Dinah

"Don't go far from camp, Dinah. It is not safe to make friends with the Canaanites."

"I understand, Mother." She did not intend to go far. But when two girls came and waved to her, she went to visit with them. They seemed very nice. When they said, "Come with us," she did.

She followed until she realized she could no longer see the camp of her father, Jacob. "I can't go any farther."

"The prince of our town thinks you're very pretty. He wants to meet you."

Dinah shook her head. "He should come to speak with my father first."

But Prince Shechem was right there. The young women from the town ran off, laughing. Dinah backed away from the prince, but he took hold of her and wouldn't let go. When she tried to scream, he covered her mouth and forced her to the ground. "I'm taking you home with me," he told her.

"Let me go to my home!" Dinah sobbed.

"You will be my wife!"

When she tried to get away, he picked her up and carried her, kicking, to where his family and friends were.

They all laughed and said, "The prince has chosen a wife for himself!" The prince took Dinah to his bedroom.

"My father and brothers will find me and take me back home."

He laughed at her. "No, they won't. I've already let them know I'm stronger than any of them by stealing you from right beneath their noses. You're in Shechem now, where I am the prince, and you belong to me." He locked her in his room.

Dinah sobbed and pounded on the door, crying out for someone to set her free so she could go home. No one opened the door.

When the prince returned, he told her that her father and her 12 brothers had agreed to let him marry her. But first he and all the men of Shechem would have to go through a ceremony. Then they would be in a lot of pain for a while. Dinah held her head in her hands. She did not want to marry a man who was unkind to her. What sort of husband would he be?

The prince left again. The next time he came back, he was bent over and moaning. "You must take care of me now. Look how I suffer because I love you."

Dinah knew better than to believe what he said. What did he know of love? He had showed her no kindness.

When all the men of Shechem were hurting too much to move, Dinah heard screams in the town. Then she heard her name.

"Dinah!" her brother Levi shouted.

"Dinah, where are you?" her brother Simeon cried out.

"Here!" She was fighting with the prince, who was trying to keep her quiet.

Levi and Simeon burst in and killed the prince with their swords. They grabbed Dinah and hurried her out of town. When they reached the camp, she ran into the arms of her mother, Leah. Her father, Jacob, patted her back and cried with her.

The next morning her father said, "We must move away from this place."

Killing the men of Shechem did not wipe away the terrible thing the prince had done to Dinah. Now no one would ever forget what had happened to her in Shechem. Dinah and her family suffered because of the prince. But the people of Shechem also suffered because of Levi's and Simeon's furious anger.

Scripture: Genesis 34:1-31

growing time

Interesting Facts

- Dinah was the only girl in Jacob's family, but she had a dozen brothers! Big families were common in those days. Boys went to school and learned their fathers' work. Girls stayed home, learning from their mothers and other women how to be a wife and mother.

- The name Dinah means "judgment." Her name was fitting because judgment came down on the men of Shechem for the way their prince treated Dinah. Judgment came to her family, too, because of what her brothers did to the men of Shechem.

Truths from God's Word

God provides families to keep us safe. They teach us God's rules and set family rules about what we can do and where we can go. God wants us to stay away from dangerous locations. But if we find ourselves in a place where we shouldn't be, God sees us through the hard times we may face there and punishes anyone who tries to hurt us.

Thinking about Dinah

Young women like Dinah were not safe unless they stayed near their families' tents. When Dinah arrived in Shechem, the prince hurt her and locked her in his room. Then her brothers came and killed all the men in Shechem. What the brothers did is called revenge. Why do you think God tells us to let him be the one to take revenge for wrongs done to us? How did Dinah's family show love for her when she returned home?

Thinking about YOUR Life

Parents and grandparents set rules to protect you. They know that not everyone who seems nice really is. How can you know if someone is trustworthy? What are some places your parents have told you not to go? Why do you think they want you to stay away from there? How might God help you if you find yourself in a place where you didn't intend to be?

Praying for Help to Obey

1. Pray that you will listen to your parents or grandparents so you will know how to stay safe.

2. Ask God to help you obey His rules and laws in the Bible, which are there to protect you.

3. If you ever accidentally find yourself in a dangerous place, pray that God will show you a way to escape.

Miriam

In all her life, Miriam had never been so angry with her younger brother, Moses. And she was an old woman now, deserving of respect! After all she had done for him, Moses was going to get married to a Cushite woman from Africa? How could he do this to her? She had been quietly upset when he had married Zipporah, who was a foreign woman from Midian. Now she was not going to keep silent.

If it were not for Miriam, Moses would not even be alive! Hadn't she been the one to watch over him as he floated down the Nile River in that basket their mother had made? And when Pharaoh's daughter had found him, who had been the one to come out of hiding? Who had told the Egyptian princess that she would need a woman to nurse the baby? Who had said she knew a woman who could do that? She had! Because Miriam had been so brave, Pharaoh's daughter had even

paid their mother to take care of Moses!

When Moses had come back to Egypt after 40 years of hiding in Midian because he had murdered an Egyptian, who had welcomed him? Miriam had! Who had encouraged everyone to listen to everything her brother said? She had! And who had led the women in playing tambourines and singing songs of praise after Moses had led all the people across the Red Sea? She had!

Moses was an old man now. She was not going to watch her brother make a fool of himself and her. She was as much a leader among the people as Moses was!

Miriam went to her other brother, Aaron. She knew better than to talk about her feelings. He might think she was jealous

and not listen to her. She knew how to make him do what she wanted. "Moses is in love with that young Cushite. We must think of the Law. We must think of the people. The woman is not one of our people, Aaron. It doesn't matter if she believes in God! She's a foreigner from Africa. A foreigner! It's a sin for Moses to marry her, and we must speak out against it. Besides, you are his older brother. You are the one who should lead the people."

Soon both Miriam and Aaron were saying bad things about their brother—things like, "Moses isn't the only leader. We're good leaders too. We can tell everyone what God has said just as Moses does." People overheard them speaking. It did not take long before the entire camp buzzed with gossip.

The Lord called for Moses, Miriam, and Aaron to appear before Him. Miriam was certain the Lord would take her side.

Hadn't she been a good helper for God from the time she was a little girl? He would know she was a better leader than her younger brother.

But the Lord was furious! "Who are you to say bad things about the man I have chosen to lead Israel?"

Miriam couldn't believe God's words. And now what was happening? Her body felt strange to her. When she looked at Aaron, she saw the fear on his face. "Your skin is covered with white spots," he said. "You have leprosy!"

She looked at her hands and cried. She was going to die of a terrible disease!

Aaron fell to his knees and cried out to his brother, "Oh, my lord! Please don't punish us for our sin. We should not have spoken against you, Moses. Please make our sister well!"

Moses prayed for Miriam. He begged God to heal her. Miriam covered her face with shame over the terrible things she had said about her brother.

The Lord did heal her, but He told her she must live outside the camp for seven days. She did a lot of thinking during that time. Before the seven days were up, she knew how wrong she had been.

When Miriam came back to the camp, she went straight to Moses and his wife. "I was wrong to say bad things about you. I am very sorry." Moses and the Cushite woman forgave her, and both were happy to call her their sister again.

Miriam never spoke another word against Moses.

Scriptures: Exodus 2:1-21; 15:20-21; Numbers 12:1-16; 20:1

growing time

Interesting Facts

- In Bible times there was no cure for leprosy. White spots went down deep into the skin. Fingers and toes would fall off because nerves were damaged and people could not feel those parts of their bodies. They would often bump their hands and feet or burn them. Some forms of leprosy are still around today in places like India, Nepal, and Africa. But now there is medicine for it.

- Cushites were from the family of Cush, who was the son of Ham and grandson of Noah. They lived in Ethiopia, a country in Africa. It is almost twice the size of the state of Texas. More than 80 languages are spoken there!

Truths from God's Word

God chooses our leaders. He wants us to respect them, especially when they are members of our family. He doesn't want us to say bad things about them. And He doesn't want us to act as if we are more important than they are.

Thinking about Miriam

When God made Moses a leader, Miriam was not kind to her younger brother. She acted as if she thought God didn't know what He was doing. She got her other brother, Aaron, and other people mad at Moses by saying bad things about him. What did God say and do that shows how angry He was with Miriam? Do you think God wanted her to die? How did He answer Moses' prayers?

Thinking about YOUR Life

Gossiping is saying unkind things about someone when the person isn't around. It always leads to trouble. Think of a time when someone gossiped about you and got you in trouble. How did it make you feel? If we gossip about our leaders and question what they are doing when they are following God, it is like saying we don't believe God knows what He is doing. How does God feel when you don't believe He has chosen good leaders?

Praying about Having Respect

1. Pray that God will show you how to respect the leaders He has given you.

2. Ask God to help you not to gossip or say bad things about anyone, especially your leaders.

3. Pray that you will not be jealous of those God has chosen to be the leaders in your family.

Caleb

The first time the Israelites came near Canaan, Moses asked one leader from each of the 12 tribes to go and see how wonderful the Promised Land was. Caleb was the one who was picked to go from the tribe of Judah.

When Caleb and the other spies went into Canaan, they found bunches of grapes so big that they needed a pole and two men to carry them!

Caleb's friend Joshua was as excited as he was. They returned with fruit from the land.

They told Moses and the other Israelites, "The land is so rich it seems to flow with milk and honey, just as the Lord said!"

But the 10 other spies were afraid. They didn't want to go back to Canaan.

"The people are strong! They are giants! We felt as small as grasshoppers next to them. They live in cities with

thick walls around them! We will all be killed if we try
to take the land."

Caleb tried to encourage the people. "The Lord
promised us the land! God does not break
His promises. We should do what God said.
We should go take the land! With God on
our side, we do not need to be afraid."

But the people would not believe. They became so angry
with Caleb and Joshua for insisting they go into the land that
they wanted to kill them!

That is when God came to their rescue and appeared to
the people. God spoke to Moses, who reported God's words to the
Israelites. "Because you didn't believe what I said, you will spend
the rest of your lives in the desert. After all of you die, Caleb and
Joshua will take your children into the land you would not enter.
I will let Caleb and Joshua do this because they
are the only ones who trusted Me."

Scripture: Numbers 13:1–14:35

growing time

Interesting Facts

- The name Caleb means "dog." At the time when the Bible was written, dogs were not pets. They ran wild, eating other animals. Caleb's name fit him because he was bold and stood up against those who opposed him.

- There really were giants living in the land of Canaan. Goliath, the giant David killed years later (see 1 Samuel 17) may have been one of their descendants. Caleb trusted God to keep him safe from the giants. Many people name their sons Caleb today, hoping they will have faith like Caleb did.

Truths from God's Word

When God promises to do something for us, He always keeps His promise. But He expects us to do the work needed to receive all that He has planned for us. He doesn't want us to be afraid, even if the people around us are.

Thinking about Caleb

Twelve spies went into the Promised Land. Two said, "Let's go!" And 10 said, "No!" Caleb and his friend Joshua were the two who stood alone against the other 10 spies and all the people of Israel. How do you suppose Caleb and Joshua felt when they found themselves in the minority—the only ones who trusted God? What do Caleb's words and actions tell you about his friendship with God? If you had been a spy, do you think you would have been afraid, or would you have agreed with Caleb and Joshua? Why?

Thinking about YOUR Life

It takes courage to believe God will keep His promises when people around you don't believe. It may be hard to stand against them and do what God wants you to do, but God promises to be with you. Is there something that is frightening you right now? Some of the bigger boys and girls at your school might be bullying the others, and everyone is afraid to stand up to them. How can you be like Caleb? How might God help you get rid of your fears?

Praying for Courage

1. Pray for courage to be like Caleb whenever you are afraid to trust God and do what He wants.

2. Ask God to help you trust Him to take care of any giant problems you are facing.

3. Pray that God will help you follow Him wherever He wants you to go and do whatever He wants you to do.

Balaam

"Great Prophet, we come from Midian and Moab in the name of King Balak to seek your help." The dusty soldiers bowed their faces to the ground.

Balaam (BAY-lum) looked at the carved boxes full of money to pay for his services. "Stand and tell me why you've come."

"King Balak has heard that those you bless are blessed and those you curse are doomed. A huge crowd of people has arrived from Egypt. King Balak fears that they will harm him and his people. The king asks that you come and curse them so that bad things will happen to them. Then perhaps King Balak will be able to drive them from his land."

The Israelites! Balaam had heard stories about these people and their God, who had opened the Red Sea so that they could walk across on dry land. He was afraid of the Israelites, but he was more afraid of their God.

Balaam looked at the money boxes. He thought of everything he could buy. "Stay here overnight," he told King Balak's soldiers. "In the morning I will tell you whatever the Lord directs me to say."

That night, God spoke to Balaam. "Do not go with these men. You are not to curse the Israelites, for I have blessed them!"

Balaam was upset because he would love to have had the money the men brought. However, he did not dare go against God. The next morning, he told the men so. Balaam watched the soldiers load the money boxes on their camels and ride away.

The king of Moab sent more soldiers! "King Balak said he will pay you well and do anything you ask of him if you will curse the people of Israel."

Balaam thought about what he could buy with all that money, but then he thought about what God had said. "Even if King Balak were to give me a palace filled with silver and gold, I am not able to do anything against God. But stay here one more night to see if the Lord has anything else to say to me." Balaam hoped God would change His mind. After all, a man had to make a living, didn't he?

"Since these men have come for you," God said that night, "get up and go with them. But be sure to do only what I tell you to do."

Balaam could not have been more pleased. He got on his donkey and set off, eager to curse the Israelites so that he could earn the money King Balak had offered. But God was upset with Balaam.

As the prophet rode along, his donkey suddenly left the road and ran down into a field. "Whoa!" Balaam shouted, "Whoa, you stupid animal!"

The soldiers laughed.

Balaam was angry because the donkey had made him look foolish. He beat the donkey with his walking stick. "Get back up on the road, you stupid beast!"

The donkey moved so tightly along the wall between the road and the field that Balaam's foot scraped against the wall and was crushed. "Move over!" Balaam beat his donkey again, harder than before.

The donkey began to shake beneath him. When the donkey lay on the ground, more people laughed.

Balaam was so angry he climbed off and beat his donkey a third time.

The donkey cried out at the blows and then looked at Balaam with sad eyes. "What have I done to make you want to beat me three times?"

Balaam shouted. "If I had a sword, I would kill you!"

"But I am the donkey you always ride. Have I ever done anything like this before?"

"No." And then Balaam thought to himself, *A donkey doesn't speak!* Balaam's anger turned to fear as he looked up and saw someone wonderful but terrifying on the road, his hand holding a sword up high. Balaam let out a scream and bowed before the angel of the Lord.

"Why did you beat your donkey three times?" the angel asked.

Balaam was too terrified to answer.

"I have come to stop you, Balaam, because I am not pleased with what you are doing. Three times the donkey saw me and tried to get away!"

"I have sinned!" Balaam said. "I did not see you standing in the road. Do you want me to go back home?"

"Go with these men, but you may say only what I tell you to say."

King Balak was waiting for him. Balaam told the king to build seven altars and give offerings to God. The king did so while Balaam went to the top of a hill. God came there and said, "Go back to Balak and tell him what I told you."

Balaam went to the king. "You brought me here, King Balak, to curse the Israelites, but how can I curse those God has blessed? All I can do is what God tells me to do!"

The king still did not give up. "You can curse some of the people at least." But Balaam would not do it.

King Balak was very angry. "Go back home!" he shouted. "I had planned to give you a lot of money. But you chose to listen to God, so you won't get it."

Scripture: Numbers 22:1–24:11

growing time

Interesting Facts

- Donkeys are from Africa. They are stronger than horses and live longer. They also don't trip or fall as easily as a horse. Donkeys can walk over rough ground and carry heavy loads. Mary rode a donkey into Bethlehem, and Jesus rode one into Jerusalem. Even though donkeys don't usually talk, God chose to speak to Balaam through his donkey!

- Balaam was not an Israelite and didn't love God like the Israelites did. But he could hear the one true God speak. He obeyed God because he knew that God is powerful. He knew that obeying God was more important than obeying King Balak.

Truths from God's Word

Other people may tempt us to do things that do not please God. But God shows us what is right to do, sometimes by sending an angel or a person who loves God.

Thinking about Balaam

Balaam was promised money to say bad things that would hurt the Israelites. He would have liked to have the money. But God had a different plan. God told Balaam to say kind words that would bless the Israelites. Balaam knew that even if he wanted to curse them (to tell about bad things that were going to happen to them), he could not say anything God did not want him to say. Why did Balaam want to curse the Israelites? Why did he choose to bless them instead?

Thinking about YOUR Life

Have you ever wanted to say mean things about someone to hurt that person? What happens when you choose to say nice things instead? Even though you can't see God or His angels around you, can you think of a time when God may have helped you say or do the right thing?

Praying for God's Help

1. Pray that God will show you which people to listen to when friends tell you to say different things.

2. Thank God for His angels, who watch over you, even though you can't see them.

3. Ask God to help you know how to follow Him, even when you can't see Him.

Daughters of Zelophehad

After 40 long years of wandering in the wilderness, the Israelites finally entered the Promised Land of Canaan. God told the leaders to divide up the land among the 12 tribes of people. Within every tribe, each man received land for his family.

But there was one family in which there was no man to get the land. The father, Zelophehad (zel-AHF-eh-had), had died in the wilderness. He never had a son, but he had five daughters: Mahlah (MAH-lah), Noah (NOH-ah), Hoglah (HAHG-lah), Milcah (MIL-kah), and Tirzah (TER-zah).

Tirzah, the youngest, cried. "What happens to us now?"

"We have no land—no place to live," Milcah said.

The girls felt sad, but they were also upset. "It is not fair for

our father's family to lose his share of land just because he had no son!"

Hoglah sat down, not knowing what to do. "We are no better than slaves among all these free men."

Noah looked at their oldest sister, Mahlah. "What are we going to do?"

"We will talk to Moses. God chose him to be our leader, and God speaks to him. We will ask him for the land that would have belonged to our father if he had lived."

The others were afraid. "Everyone will be against us! You know women are never allowed to inherit land from their father. The inheritance always goes to a man—to a son or brother."

Mahlah stood firm. "Have courage! God always does what is right and fair. Moses will ask God what can be done for us, and we will trust in the Lord. Not once did God leave us alone in the wilderness. Hasn't God always taken care of us?"

"Yes!"

"Then let us go to Moses and have faith that God will take care of us now."

The five young women went to discuss their problem with Moses and the other leaders. "Our father died in the wilderness without leaving any sons. Why should our family not get land just because he had no sons? Give us the property that belongs to us."

The men were shocked at such a bold request, but Moses went to the Lord and asked Him what to do.

The Lord answered, "The daughters of Zelophehad are right. You must give them, as well as their father's other relatives, an inheritance of land. I want them to have the property that would have been given to their father. And let everyone know that if a man dies and has no sons, everything that was his is to go to his daughters."

Moses went back to the five young women. Everyone in camp gathered to hear what Moses had learned from God. And Moses told them exactly what the Lord had said. No longer would the Israelites be allowed to follow old customs. They were to follow God, who loved and provided for all His people—men and women alike!

Laughing and crying in joy, the girls praised God. They were thankful that God cared about them. And they knew they could always trust God to do what was right.

Some of the people worried that the land might fall into the wrong hands if any of the women married a man who was not from their tribe. So Moses said, "Be certain that each of you marries a man from the tribe of Manasseh (ma-NA-suh). That way the land will stay in your family."

"We will do that," promised Mahlah, Noah, Hoglah, Milcah, and Tirzah. The five daughters followed Moses' instructions, and the land they inherited stayed in their family.

Scriptures: Numbers 27:1-11; 36:1-12; Joshua 17:3-6

growing time

Interesting Facts

- Women have not always had the same rights as men. They have been treated poorly, as if they were not important. In some countries today, women are still treated that way. The leaders of those countries need to learn from the Bible how God wants women to be treated.

- Noah can be a name for a man or a woman. As a man's name—like Noah who built the ark—it means "rest" or "comfort." As a woman's name—like in this story—it means "motion." Zelophehad's daughter Noah and her sisters set into motion some new laws for women!

Truths from God's Word

God is fair. He always does what is right for boys and girls, men and women. God will never forget about us, and He will give us the courage to ask for help when we need it.

Thinking about the Daughters of Zelophehad

The five young women felt as if God had forgotten about them after their father died. Land was supposed to pass down only from a father to a son. There was nothing in the laws about passing land from a father to his daughters. The five sisters were worried about asking the leaders to give them the land, but they knew they had to ask those men anyway. Why do you think they were scared? How did God take care of them? What might have happened if they hadn't asked for the land?

Thinking about YOUR Life

God will always provide the things you need. But you may have to ask for help, just as the women in the Bible story did. Have you ever been scared to ask for something you needed? What was it? Did you ask, and if you did, was the answer a yes or a no? Why? (Think about whether you really needed what you asked for.) Don't be afraid to ask for help when you think you are being left out or not getting what you should have.

Praying for Things You Need

1. Ask God to help you believe He will always remember you and take care of you.

2. Pray for courage to ask for the things you need.

3. Ask God to give you wisdom so you'll understand which things you need and which things you would like to have but don't really need.

Deborah

During the time when the people of Israel were slaves to Canaan's King Jabin (JAY-bin), God called a woman to be judge over His people. Her name was Deborah. She lived between the towns of Ramah and Bethel.

Every day Deborah sat under the shade of a palm tree and listened to the Israelite people argue with one another. She would hear both sides of each case. Then she would decide who was right, based on the Law God had given His people. The Israelites trusted her because God had given her great wisdom.

One day God told her to send for Barak (BEAR-rack),

one of the men from her country. Barak came quickly, and Deborah told him, "This is what the Lord wants you to do. Gather 10,000 warriors and bring them to fight at Mount Tabor (TAY-ber). God will make sure that Sisera (SIS-er-uh), King Jabin's army commander, comes to the Kishon (KEY-shon) River. And God will give you victory over him!"

Barak was afraid! Sisera was a powerful man with a huge army. He had tens of thousands of well-equipped and trained soldiers. He also had 900 iron chariots. These heavy horse-drawn carts carried men who could use their bows and arrows to kill more than 10,000 people! Barak did not believe he could win a battle against these fighters. So he said, "I will go, Deborah, but only if you go with me!"

Deborah understood then that Barak did not have faith in God. He did not believe God's promise to give Israel success. "I will go with you, Barak," said Deborah. "But you will receive no honor. God will bring victory over Sisera through the work of a woman."

Everyone thought that woman would be Deborah, but there was a surprise ahead!

That very day, Deborah went with Barak. They gathered the 10,000 warriors, and Deborah marched with Barak and the fighting men to Mount Tabor.

When Sisera heard they were coming, he brought his huge army and all his chariots to the Kishon River, just as God said he would. The battle began! But it did not go badly for Barak, as he had expected it would. And it didn't go well for Sisera, as he had expected.

God fought for Israel! He caused Sisera and his men not to know what they were doing. Sisera began to panic! He was so scared that he jumped from his chariot and ran away! Then God helped Barak and Deborah destroy the entire Canaanite army.

A woman named Jael (JAY-el) invited Sisera to hide in her tent. When he came inside, she gave him warm milk and a blanket so that he would fall asleep. Then she took a hammer and tent peg and killed Sisera.

Now the commander of the enemy army was dead, along with all his soldiers. The war was over! The Israelites would no longer need to worry about the Canaanites, who had made life difficult for them for 20 years. They were free!

Deborah wrote a song about what had happened and sang it to all the people. She gave honor to Jael, singing about how brave she was. Jael had killed the Canaanite army commander and brought the war to an end.

Scripture: Judges 4–5

growing time

Interesting Facts

- A chariot is like a wagon or cart with two wheels, pulled by two horses. In Bible times, one man would stand at the front of a chariot, directing the horses. Another man would have a weapon to fight off enemies. A soldier walking nearby would find it hard to fight against someone in a chariot.

- A tent peg is a huge, thick nail used to fasten a tent to the ground. Tent pegs hold a tent in place so it won't fall over.

Truths from God's Word

God chooses leaders who are wise and brave. Sometimes He gives instructions that leaders don't understand. If they trust Him, they will follow His directions anyway, and He will watch over them. God wants everyone to listen to wise leaders and do what they say.

Thinking about Deborah

Deborah had a powerful job. She was a wise judge who settled arguments between the people of her country. She was also a prophet who got messages from God. What message did she give Barak? How did he reply? What might have happened if Deborah had been afraid to go into battle? Why was she so brave? How did Deborah and Jael help the people of Israel?

Thinking about YOUR Life

God has a purpose for you. Maybe He wants you to be a leader some of the time. Much of the time He will want you to be a follower. When God shows you what He would like you to do, you need to be ready to listen and obey. How can you be sure that God is the one who wants you to do these things? (Hint: The Bible shows us how to live.) Name some of your leaders at home, at school, at church, in your city, and in your country. How can you be a good follower of each leader? When it's your turn to be a leader, how can God make you wise and brave?

Praying about Leading and Following

1. Ask God to help you listen and obey as you follow Him and other leaders He has given you.

2. Pray for your leaders, asking God to make them wise and brave.

3. Pray that you will be wise and brave when God chooses you to be a leader.

Gideon worked as fast as he could, pitching wheat into the air to separate the grain from the shell, called the chaff. He needed to finish the work and hide the wheat before the Midianites (MIH-dee-un-nights) discovered that the fields had produced a crop. Those people had no mercy! They came in large groups, riding their camels, and took away everything valuable that the Israelites had.

As Gideon worked, he suddenly noticed someone sitting under an oak tree. He didn't know it was the angel of the Lord.

"Mighty hero!" the angel said. "The Lord is with you." Gideon did not understand.

He asked, "Sir, if the Lord is with us, why do the Midianites take everything we have?" Gideon looked around, wondering when the enemy would come. He still had a lot of work left to do. "The Lord has left us!"

"I am sending you to rescue Israel," said the angel. Gideon realized now that this must be an angel bringing him a message from the Lord.

"Me?!" Gideon wondered why the Lord would send him. What could he do against an army of Midianite warriors? "My family is the smallest in the country, and I am the least important person among them!"

"I will be with you," the angel said. "And you will destroy all the Midianites."

Gideon shook his head. He did not know anything about fighting. He was a farmer. The Midianites were trained warriors. "Show me a sign that the Lord is saying this to me," Gideon said. "But wait while I go home and make a food offering."

Gideon cooked goat meat, baked fresh bread, and made soup. When he came back, the angel was waiting for him.

"Put the meat and bread on this rock," the angel told him, "and pour the soup over it." After Gideon did this, the angel touched the food with his walking stick, and the food burst into flames! Then the angel disappeared.

Gideon cried out in fear. He understood now that he had seen the Lord, and he had been taught that no one saw the Lord without dying.

"Do not be afraid. You will not die," the Lord said.

Gideon looked around but saw no one. Yet he could hear God's voice. The Lord told Gideon what to do. Gideon was still afraid, but he obeyed.

Gideon destroyed all the idols that had been made for worshipping pretend gods. He built an altar for the Lord and placed an offering on it.

When God told Gideon it was time to fight the Midianites, Gideon was more afraid than ever. Again he told the Lord, "Give me a sign. I will put a piece of wool outside during the night. If it is wet and the ground is dry in the morning, I will go to war with your help." In the morning, the wool was wet and the ground was dry.

Gideon was still afraid, so he asked God for another sign. "Let the ground be wet, but make the wool dry tomorrow morning." The Lord was very patient with Gideon and did what he asked. Gideon was finally sure that the Lord was with him and would help him win the war.

He called all the men of Israel to be in his army. When they left for war, the Lord told Gideon there were too many men— 32,000 of them! God wanted the people to realize that they would win because of His strength, not because of the number of men in their army. He told Gideon to send home all the men who were afraid. So 22,000 left. The Lord said there were still too many men. By the time the Lord finished sending men home, there were only 300 men left to fight against thousands of Midianites!

God helped Gideon know what to do. Gideon told his men to stand on the hills around the Midianite camp. He said, "Blow your rams' horns and shout! Then break the clay jars with the torches inside. Hold the burning torches high."

When the Midianites heard the horns and shouting and saw the torches burning, they thought a huge army had come against them. They were terrified. They ran in all directions. They even started fighting and killing one another.

After that day, Gideon was considered a great hero in Israel, but it was really God who had won the battle. Gideon told the people, "It is the Lord who will rule over you!"

Scriptures: Judges 6:3–7:22; 8:22-23

growing time

Interesting Facts

- People in Israel sometimes ride camels instead of horses. Camels can live in dry areas, such as deserts, where horses would not survive. They can drink up to 20 gallons of water at a time. The water is stored in their blood, not in their humps. A camel's hump stores fat.

- The Midianites were relatives of Moses' first wife, Zipporah, but later became enemies of Israel.

Truths from God's Word

God gives different jobs to different people. Sometimes the work He gives us seems too hard.
He is pleased when we trust and obey Him anyway.

Thinking about Gideon

All the Israelites were abused by Midianite thieves who stole their animals and food. But God sent an angel to call just one scared farmer to drive these enemies from the land. Gideon did not believe the angel at first. But God showed Gideon that He was there with him by doing two "woolly" miracles. God knew that Gideon felt he was just a small, not-very-important person who could not do anything big. But when Gideon obeyed God, finally trusting God to help him, how did God help him become useful in a big way?

Thinking about YOUR Life

Have you ever felt afraid to try something? Have you felt too small to help anyone? How can you work with God to do big things?

Praying about Doing God's Will

1. Pray that God will give you the strength to do what He wants—to do His will—even when you feel too small to help.

2. Pray that God will show you how to do what He wants.

3. If you are afraid, ask God to help you do big things for Him anyway.

Naomi

"Can't we stay here in Bethlehem?" Naomi asked her husband. "We have family and friends. Rain will come someday. Then crops will grow again and the famine will end."

"I don't want to wait, Naomi. If we go to Moab now, we can take plenty with us to have a good life there. But soon there will be very little food to eat in Bethlehem."

But what good would life be without God?

Naomi worried about their two sons. She knew the Moabites worshipped idols, but Elimelech (eh-LIM-uh-lek) did not seem to be afraid that his sons would ever do that. So they packed their belongings and moved to Moab. Naomi's husband began a business there.

The years passed, and Naomi never stopped listening for any news from the land of Israel.

She missed her family and friends. She missed going to Jerusalem to worship the Lord. Her sons were growing up and would each need a wife soon. But even though the famine was over, Naomi's husband made no plans to return to Israel.

Then Elimelech died, leaving Naomi alone with her two sons. She tried to talk them into going back to Israel, but they said Moab was their home. What about wives? "We have each chosen our own wife among the girls here."

Naomi was sad, but she liked Orpah and Ruth when she met them. So she treated them as if they were her own daughters. She prayed for them every day and told them all about the Lord. Orpah listened just to be polite, but Ruth wanted to hear every word.

Then something else sad happened to Naomi. Both of her sons became sick and died. "God has left me alone!" She had lost everything that was important to her. Naomi had no way to make a living, so she would have to beg for everything she needed to stay alive.

"I'm going home to Bethlehem," Naomi said. At least there, if she starved to death, she would be among her own people.

Ruth put her arms around her mother-in-law. "We'll go with you!" Orpah agreed.

"No! You have families here. Go home to them. They will find a new husband for each of you."

Orpah took Naomi's advice and went home, but Ruth refused to leave Naomi. "I will go where you go. I will stay

where you stay. Your people will become my people, and your God will become my God."

Naomi left Moab and returned to Bethlehem, taking Ruth with her. When they arrived, Naomi learned her mother and father and brothers and sisters had all died. Though she had other relatives, she did not ask them for help. And no one offered her any.

Ruth comforted her mother-in-law. "I will go and gather grain that is left over from the fields being harvested. We will have enough to eat for a long time."

"The landowners will not be kind to you, because you are a woman from Moab."

"The Lord our God will protect me and provide what we need."

And the Lord did! The first day Ruth went into the fields, she met Boaz (BOH-az), a wealthy landowner who loved God. He found out who Ruth was and how kind she had been to Naomi. So Boaz treated her kindly.

When Ruth told Naomi about Boaz, Naomi was filled with hope. She could tell that Boaz liked Ruth very much! "He is a relative of my husband, who died. Do exactly what I say, Ruth, and everything will be fine!" She told Ruth to dress in her finest clothes and go to the threshing floor, where the men worked and celebrated the harvest. "Sleep at Boaz's feet and let him know when he awakens that you would be happy to marry him. He will tell you what to do then."

Ruth obeyed.

Boaz happily married Ruth, and they had a son, Obed (OH-bed). Boaz took back Elimelech's land and gave it to Obed. After that, Elimelech's family always had their own property.

Naomi loved her grandson, Obed. She took care of him as if he were her own son. All her friends were happy with her. "You have a family again because of Ruth. She is better than seven sons!"

Naomi laughed with joy as she held baby Obed. "God did not forget me." She knew God had given her and Ruth blessings far beyond anything they ever could have expected!

Scripture: The book of Ruth

growing time

Interesting Facts

- A threshing floor is the place where wheat, which can be made into flour, is separated from the chaff or straw, which cannot be eaten. The men who beat the grain to separate it would sleep on the threshing floor because they would work there again in the morning.

- A redeemer is someone who saves you when you can't take care of yourself. This person sets you free, often by taking your place and doing what you can't do yourself. Boaz was a redeemer for Ruth and for Naomi. Jesus is the most important Redeemer of all. He came to redeem or save all of us from our sins.

Truths from God's Word

Sometimes sad things happen to people, even to those who love God. But God always sends someone to comfort and help those who are sad. It may be a longtime friend, a family member, or a person from another country. It is often the last person we would expect.

Thinking about Naomi

Naomi felt as if God had left her all alone because her husband and sons had died. But God provided a daughter-in-law named Ruth to comfort and help her. Ruth was from a country where the people did not believe in God, but He became her God. What might have happened to Naomi if she had not let Ruth go back to Israel with her? After Ruth met Boaz, what did Naomi ask Ruth to do? How did Boaz help to save the family of Elimelech (Naomi's husband, who had died)?

Thinking about YOUR Life

It may seem at times that God has left you alone, but He never will. He provides for you in ways that you can see and in a lot of ways that you can't see. Have you ever felt sad? Maybe someone in your family or someone you knew well died. Who did God put in your life to comfort you and help you through that? Look at the people around you and think about some ways they helped you when you were sad or needed help.

Praying about Things You Need

1. Thank God for the ways He has always provided for your needs.

2. Ask God to send someone to help you whenever you feel sad.

3. Pray that you will be able to help your family members when they need you.

${\Large \text{A}}$bigail could hear the party going on. Her husband, Nabal (NAY-bul), was drunk again and boasting about the number of sheep and goats he owned. He was a rich man but a foolish one who never gave glory to God for anything! Abigail shook her head and went back to her chores.

One of her husband's shepherds ran toward her.

"Mistress! We're in terrible trouble!"

"What's happened?"

"David sent 10 men asking for supplies for his warriors, and Nabal yelled at them. He said unkind things about David and his men. They were kind to us when we were out in the wilderness with our flocks of sheep. Not one animal was lost while they were with us! And now, Nabal shows no thankfulness! We're all afraid David will come to get back at Nabal!"

Abigail knew that men of war often let their anger get out of control, and David had been at war with his enemies for years. Not only that, but the prophet Samuel said that God wanted David to be the next king. That made King Saul very jealous, and now David had to try to stay safe so that Saul could not kill him!

As usual, her husband, Nabal, had spoken without thinking. It was up to her to save her husband and the shepherds.

Abigail thought quickly and called all her servants together. "Hurry! Pack every loaf of bread you can find. Pack wine, meat and grain, raisins and fig cakes, and load the supplies into carts. I will ride out ahead of you and try to stop David from fighting us."

"But he will kill you, Mistress!"

"My life is in God's hands."

David was known for being a man who loved God. It is God's job to correct people for doing what is wrong. But if Abigail was unable to stop him, David might hurt her husband by trying to correct Nabal himself. She had to get David's attention long enough to talk him out of doing something he would feel bad about later.

David and 400 of his warriors rode toward her. She prayed as she rode her donkey down the middle of the road, blocking David and his army. She knew that in their anger, they could ride right over her!

David stopped and glared at her. There was no smile on his face.

"I am Abigail, the wife of Nabal. Please forgive me." She spoke quickly and from her heart. She took blame for not knowing that David had sent 10 of his men for food and other things they needed. As the carts rumbled up behind her, she offered David and his men the supplies Nabal had refused to give them. "The Lord has picked you to be our next king. Please do not sin against the Lord our God by trying to get even with Nabal, for he is a foolish man."

David listened to Abigail. Slowly, a smile began to spread across his face. "I thank God that you came here. If you had not been brave enough to come, I would have murdered your husband and every man in your camp."

He accepted the supplies and rode away.

Abigail returned home, glad that David was no longer angry. Nabal was still drunk, so she waited until the next day when he was sober to tell him all that had happened. Then Nabal became so upset that he had a stroke! A few days later, he died.

When David heard, he knew Abigail was now a widow who needed help. Evil men might steal all her husband's property. So he sent some more of his men with a message for Abigail. He said he wanted to marry her.

Abigail said yes! She could not have been happier, because she knew God was giving her a godly husband. One day he would be king!

Scripture: 1 Samuel 25:1-44

growing time

Interesting Facts

- When Abigail married David, she was one of three wives. By the time David died, he had at least eight wives. But that was not God's best plan. From the beginning, God said that a marriage is between two people—one man and one woman (see Genesis 2:24). And Jesus said that a husband and wife should stay together as long as they live (see Matthew 5:31-32).

- Nabal lived in an area named Maon, which means "place of sin." Do you think it was named that before or after Nabal?

Truths from God's Word

Sometimes we have to make up for the bad things other people do. God watches over us and helps us to be brave when we try to make things right.

Thinking about Abigail

Abigail took a big risk in going out to meet David. She trusted God to keep her safe, and He did. Abigail hadn't done anything wrong but knew that she was the only one who could make things right. Because she was brave, everyone in her family group was safe. How do you think Abigail felt as she went out to face an entire army by herself?

Thinking about YOUR Life

Although you will probably never have to stand up to an army, there will be times in your life when you will have to stand alone. Was there ever a time when you had to stand up for others who couldn't help themselves? Have you ever had to help keep a friend safe who couldn't see the danger in what he or she was doing? Name other times when your help might be necessary.

Praying about Making Things Right

1. Pray that you will be brave enough to do what is right when others have done something wrong.

2. Ask God to give you the words to say when you have to stand alone and to make you brave so you will say them.

3. Pray that God will open others' ears to hear what He has to say through you.

Queen of Sheba

The young queen of Sheba wanted more than anything else to know the difference between good and evil so that she could rule her people wisely. But whenever she asked her helpers for advice, she knew they said only what they thought she wanted to hear. She could not learn anything that way! So she listened to all that went on around her, hoping she would learn from her people. But that did not work either. The people wanted their queen to help them be wise.

One day the queen heard some men talking about a king who ruled the distant land of Israel with great wisdom. They were traders who had come to trade perfumes, oils, copper, and iron for gold and spices. She called for them. "Tell me more about this king of Israel."

They were afraid that the queen was upset. So they bowed their faces to the ground. "We did not mean to say anything that would make you seem less important than King Solomon, your majesty."

"Do not be afraid. I just want to know about this king."

"He rules Israel," one said.

"He is the greatest man in the world," said the other.

"What makes him so great?" She wanted to know.

"He knows everything! And he is richer than any other king or queen."

The queen of Sheba cared nothing about wealth. She had more than enough money. But she did long to have true wisdom so she would always know the best thing to do. "I would like to meet this king and see for myself if what you say is true!" She ordered her officials to gather a group of men with animals that would carry the best gifts her country had to offer. Then she set off for Jerusalem, the capital city of Israel.

The journey was long and difficult, through land that was rocky, hot, and dry.

When the queen of Sheba arrived, she received a royal welcome at King Solomon's palace. She had never seen such a huge, beautiful place. Even the king's officials drank from golden cups!

King Solomon was everything she had been told he was. When he spoke, everyone listened. He taught about the Lord God of heaven and earth. He talked about the Law this great God had given the Israelites. Solomon knew all about birds and animals. Most of all, he understood people. He often spoke in proverbs, and these short sayings were easy to remember.

When the queen of Sheba asked King Solomon many difficult questions about God and how to rule people, King Solomon answered all of them. "To have wisdom, you must first be filled with wonder when you think about God," he told her. "Trust in the Lord with all your heart, and don't count on your own ability to understand things. Let Him direct you, and He will show you what's right to do."

"Truly God has made you the wisest man on earth! Your God is great indeed!"

The queen of Sheba gave King Solomon gold, spices, and jewels, but she knew she had received something greater from him: knowledge of the living God. He was a God she could choose to worship from that day on.

Scripture: 1 Kings 10:1-13; Proverbs 1:7; 3:5-6

growing time

Interesting Facts

- Sheba was a kingdom probably in what is now Yemen, a country south of Saudi Arabia. Men led caravans (long lines) of camels through the Arabian Desert from Sheba to Israel and farther north. These traders took products to sell and brought back other kinds of goods they bought.

- The queen of Sheba gave King Solomon 120 talents of gold—about 9,000 pounds. One talent was 75 pounds. (How much do you weigh?) Today 120 talents is worth more than 50 million dollars. That's a lot of money!

- The spices the queen gave Solomon might have included frankincense and myrrh, which the wise men also gave to Jesus many years later. Both spices come from tree sap and have a sweet smell. Myrrh also can kill bacteria. And frankincense can be made into a black paint.

Truths from God's Word

People who want to be wise must first want to know God and learn to trust Him. God is pleased when people look for a wise person who can teach them about God.

Thinking about the Queen of Sheba

The queen of Sheba wanted wisdom and knowledge from King Solomon. She was not jealous that Solomon was greater than she. What was the most important thing she learned from Solomon? The queen of Sheba learned all about the God of Israel. Do you think she chose to trust and obey Him? If she did, how would that have helped her become wise?

Thinking about YOUR Life

There are many books you can read to become wise and full of knowledge. The best book to read to get wisdom from God is the Bible. Do you read the Bible regularly? What have you learned from it? Do you know wise people who can help you learn about God and what the Bible says about Him? Who? What have they taught you about trusting and obeying God?

Praying for Wisdom

1. Pray that God will give you the wisdom not only to learn about Him but also to trust and obey Him.

2. Ask God to help you find people who can help you become a wise follower of Him.

3. Pray that God will show you how to share with others the wisdom and knowledge you have about Him.

Jehoiada

Jehoiada (jee-HOI-uh-duh), a priest in the Temple of the Lord, saw his wife running toward him with a baby in her arms. "What's wrong, Jehosheba (jee-HOSH-eh-bah)?"

Eyes wide, cheeks streaked with tears, she gasped. "King Ahaziah (ay-haz-I-uh) is dead, and his mother is murdering his sons so she can be the queen!" Jehosheba held the baby close. "I brought Joash (JO-ash) here as quickly as I could." She sobbed. "Oh, Jehoiada. The baby's grandmother, Athaliah (ath-uh-LI-uh), is a crazy woman! Can you

imagine someone killing all her grandsons to make herself queen? What are we going to do?"

Jehoiada thought quickly. "There is only one thing to do: keep Joash safe. He must be the next king." Jehoiada took the baby inside the Temple and kept him well hidden in a bedroom there.

Joash's wicked grandmother, Athaliah, did make herself queen and ruled over the people. She built temples and made altars where people could worship false gods. She put idols everywhere! She even paid false priests to lead the people away from the Lord!

Jehoiada kept Joash safe. The priest spent hours with the boy every day, caring for him and teaching him. He loved Joash as much as if the boy had been his own son. Jehoiada wanted to train the child to be a good king. "You must learn the Law of God, Joash. Love the Lord with all your heart, mind, soul, and strength. God will direct your steps, and you will be able to rule our people wisely."

When Joash was seven years old, Jehoiada called the captains of the army to the Temple. They came quickly because they had great respect for this man of God. Jehoiada told the captains it was time for Joash to become the king.

The captains gathered many leaders. Then Jehoiada brought Joash out to them and said, "Surround Joash." Jehoiada gave the men spears and shields that had belonged to King David. "Keep the true ruler of Judah safe!"

Jehoiada took Joash outside and stood him beside one of the large pillars of the Temple. There he put a crown on Joash and made the seven-year-old boy the king of Judah.

The people cheered and shouted, "Long live the king!"

Jehoiada sent soldiers after Athaliah. Now it was her turn to die for murdering her grandsons. The people tore down the temples to false gods, smashed the altars and idols, and killed the priests the queen had hired to lead her people into sin.

For as long as Jehoiada lived, he showed Joash how to be a good king. And as long as Jehoiada lived, King Joash followed the Lord and ruled wisely.

Scriptures: Deuteronomy 6:5; 2 Kings 11–12; 2 Chronicles 22:10-12; 23:1–24:25

growing time

Interesting Facts

- After King Joash grew up, he had the Temple repaired. This was the Temple that Solomon had built more than 120 years before Joash became king. Not only was the Temple old, but it had not been taken care of when evil kings and queens had ruled the land. Joash had a large treasure chest made, and people filled it up many times with coins to pay for repairs.

- King Joash forgot the things he had learned about God from Jehoiada after the priest died. The king had Jehoiada's son stoned for telling people that they were sinning against God.

Truths from God's Word

God is pleased when people do what they can to help others learn to follow Him. God wants those who learn to obey Him to keep on obeying, even when their teachers are no longer around. God knows that if we love Him, we will always try to do what He wants.

Thinking about Jehoiada

God planned for Jehoiada, the priest, to teach and care for the future king. Jehoiada had to lead the army in overthrowing the evil Athaliah and placing Joash on the throne. Jehoiada did what God wanted when he raised the child Joash, who was a good king as long as the priest lived. Why do you think the king stopped following God after Jehoiada died? Do you think that Jehoiada's time with Joash was wasted, since Joash didn't always do what was right? Why or why not?

Thinking about YOUR Life

Many people teach you and look after you. Name some things your parents and teachers have told you that God wants you to do. They want you to do what is right, but they can't always be with you. How do you behave when they aren't around? Do you have any habits you need to break? Who will help you with that? The way you act can change the way others act too—your brother or sister, your friends, and even people you don't know. What are some things you can do to show them the right way to live?

Praying about Following God

1. Ask God to help you learn from your parents and teachers how to follow Him.

2. Pray that you will always try to do what is right, even when no one is watching.

3. Thank God for the people who love you and teach you and help keep you safe.

Hezekiah

Hezekiah (heh-zeh-KI-uh) became king of Judah around 100 years after Joash had been king. Hezekiah was the best king Judah ever had. He wanted to please the Lord more than anything else. So he broke apart the bronze serpent the people worshipped. He tore down the pagan altars and taught his people to worship only the Lord.

And the Lord was with King Hezekiah. When he fought the powerful Philistines (FIH-lis-teens), the Lord helped him win!

But the king of Assyria (uh-SEER-ee-ah) came to the northern land of Israel and surrounded the city of Samaria. He took many Israelites away as slaves.

Then he turned his anger upon Judah, where Hezekiah ruled, and took all the strong cities except Jerusalem.

Hoping to make the Assyrian king go away, King Hezekiah gave him all the silver and gold from the Temple. But the greedy Assyrian wanted more! He ordered his army commander to take everything! The commander stood outside Jerusalem's wall and shouted to the people inside, "Do not believe King Hezekiah when he says the Lord will save you! None of the nations have been able to save themselves from us!"

Though they were afraid, the people obeyed King Hezekiah and stood silent. The king tore his clothes and covered himself with a rough cloth like burlap called sackcloth. He sent some of his leaders to the prophet Isaiah, asking him to pray for the people of Jerusalem.

The leaders came back with this message from Isaiah:

"The Lord says that you are not to be afraid. He will take care of the Assyrian king."

But the king of Assyria sent a message to Hezekiah, telling him not to believe God.

Hezekiah went to the Temple and prayed, "God of Israel, You alone are God of all the kingdoms of the earth! We are facing a terrible enemy. Help us, Lord, so that all the kingdoms on earth may know that you alone are God!"

God told Isaiah to tell King Hezekiah, "The king of Assyria and his army will not get into Jerusalem! I, the Lord, will keep the city safe."

Then God sent the angel of the Lord to destroy the Assyrian army! When the king of Assyria got up in the morning, he found thousands of dead soldiers. Terrified, he rushed back to the city of Nineveh (NIN-eh-vuh) in the land of Assyria. There, two of his own people killed him.

Scriptures: 2 Kings 18–19; 2 Chronicles 29:1-2; 31:1-3; 32:9-23

growing time

Interesting Facts

- When an enemy army surrounds a city, it is called a siege. The enemy will not let the people out to get food or water. They stay until the people inside give up or die.

- Hezekiah built a tunnel under the city of Jerusalem so that the people could always get water, even if they were under siege. His tunnel is still there today. Look up "Hezekiah's tunnel" on the Internet to see pictures of it.

Truths from God's Word

If we want to obey God, we may find we have enemies who try to scare us. But God will give us people to show us He is there to help us. God will also listen to our prayers and help take care of our enemies for us.

Thinking about Hezekiah

King Hezekiah was a wise king. He stood firm and didn't resort to yelling meaningless threats back to his enemies who were outside the city walls. He listened to what God said and then obeyed Him. Because he listened to God, Hezekiah didn't have to fight the Assyrian army. God did it for him! How do you think Hezekiah felt when the Assyrians were yelling that he was going to die? What are two things Hezekiah did to find out if God was going to help him?

Thinking about YOUR Life

It's easy to get discouraged when people all around us are saying that we will fail. We need to listen to God and not to people who try to frighten us. Have you ever had to walk away from someone who was being mean to you? How did that feel? Even if we have "enemies" who never seem to be quiet, we can choose to do what God wants us to do. How do you escape from your enemies and keep other people from bothering you when they try to scare you?

Praying for Help When You're Afraid

1. Pray that you will stand firm in doing what is right, even if others try to stop you.

2. Ask the Lord to show you that He is on your side.

3. Pray that God will show you a way to escape your enemies when they seem to be all around you.

Job (JOHB)

All the angels gathered before the Lord in heaven, even Satan, the angel who had become God's enemy. Satan spoke to God. "Look at the people You created. Not one of them truly worships You!"

"Think about Job," God said. "He does nothing wrong. He worships Me and stays away from evil."

"That's because You have blessed him with a big family and great wealth!" Satan argued. "You have given him everything, from children to land. Take all that away and he will say bad things about You to Your face!"

"Go and test him," God said.

"Do as you want with him, only do not kill him."
Now Satan would learn that a man like Job worships God even when things aren't going well for him.

Satan began making bad things happen to Job. First some men took away all his oxen and donkeys and killed his farm workers. Then fire burned up Job's sheep and shepherds. Robbers stole his camels and killed his servants. Finally, Satan sent a windstorm to crush the house where Job's children were having a party. All 10 of Job's children died—seven boys and three girls!

Crying and tearing his robe, Job bowed his head and prayed. "The Lord gives and the Lord takes away. Blessed be the name of the Lord."

God looked down at Job and told Satan, "You see now that people worship me for who I am, not just to receive blessings from Me. My servant Job is the finest man on earth."

Satan was furious! He yelled at God. "A man will curse You to Your face when he is in pain and wants to die!"

So God let Satan give Job painful boils. These sores covered him from his feet to his head. Job cried in pain. He went outside the city and sat in a garbage dump. When Job still did not curse God, Satan turned Job's wife against him. She felt bad because all her children had died. "Job, how can you still have faith in God? Look how you suffer! Curse God and die!"

Angry, Job shook his head. "Should we accept only good things from God, and not bad? Even if God kills me, I will trust in Him!"

Only four of Job's friends came to comfort him: Bildad (BILL-dad), Zophar (ZOH-far), Eliphaz (EL-ee-fahz), and the youngest, Elihu (ee-LIE-hyoo). For seven days, they said nothing. Then they started to talk . . . and talk . . . and talk. They tried to come up with some reason for Job's suffering.

Bildad told Job he must have sinned. "It is right for you to suffer for something you did wrong!"

Job said he had done nothing wrong.

"Only the guilty suffer," Zophar insisted.

Even Eliphaz lied and said Job had sent people away who needed help.

Job did not understand why God had handed him over to these unkind friends. "God knows I have done no wrong. He will take my side. My Redeemer, who will save me, lives. Someday He will take His place on the earth!"

Elihu, the youngest, tried to make everyone believe he was wiser than the other three friends. He spoke for a long time. At least he felt sorry for Job and talked about how great God is.

All this talk just made Job cry, though, and wish he had never been born. He said God had become his enemy. He didn't know Satan was the one who had caused all his suffering.

Finally, God stopped the four men from talking. He asked Job one question after another. Job needed to learn that God is in control, even when people don't understand what is happening.

Job was sorry he had questioned God. "You can do all things, Lord. You are too wonderful for words. Teach me."

Then God told Job's friends, "I am angry with you! Job will pray for you, and I will listen to him. I won't do to you what you deserve!"

After that, God blessed Job by doing many kind things for him. God gave Job twice as many animals as he had before, and many more farm workers and servants. Family and friends gave him gifts. Job and his wife had 10 more children—seven sons and three daughters. Job lived 140 years after everything was given back to him. He saw his sons and daughters grow up and marry. He saw his grandsons and their children and grandchildren grow up!

God had allowed Satan to test Job. And Job had passed his test. He kept his faith in God, no matter what Satan did to him.

Scripture: The book of Job

growing time

Interesting Facts

- The Bible says that in the first part of his life Job had 7,000 sheep, 3,000 camels, 500 teams of oxen, and 500 donkeys! Can you imagine having that many animals? And after everything Job went through, the Lord blessed him with twice that number of animals!

- Did you know that Satan was once an angel in God's Kingdom? But Satan wanted to be just as important as God. He wanted people to worship him. God could not allow Satan to stay in heaven. So now everyone must decide whether to follow God, who is loving and kind, or Satan, who is evil and unkind.

Truths from God's Word

Sometimes God allows people to suffer so that they will learn to trust Him no matter what happens. Satan wants people to get upset with God and stop worshipping Him. It's important not to listen to Satan.

Thinking about Job

Job didn't know why he was suffering. He only knew that cursing God by saying bad things about Him would not help him. He chose to believe that God loved him and was going to save him someday. Having faith in God can give hope and comfort. How do you think Job felt while he was suffering? How do you think he felt after his suffering was over?

Thinking about YOUR Life

People sometimes put blame where it doesn't belong. Has anyone ever told you that you were going through a tough time because God was mad at you? Did you think it was true? Why? After reading the story of Job, what are your thoughts about why God sometimes lets people suffer? How can you show Him you trust Him the next time you go through a hard time?

Praying about Being Faithful to God

1. Ask God to help you never stop worshipping Him, even if things aren't going well for you.

2. Pray for wisdom to know that Satan is the enemy.

3. Thank God for always understanding how you feel.

4. Ask God to show you how to be a good friend to others who need to be comforted.

Amos was a shepherd who lived in Judah in the town of Tekoa (teh-KOH-ah). One day God spoke to him and showed him visions, which were like pictures in his mind. He was awake, but it was as if he were dreaming about what God was going to do to the people in countries surrounding Israel and Judah.

The city of Damascus (duh-MAS-kus) would be destroyed because of the cruel way their people treated God's people in Gilead (GIL-ee-ud). The cities of Gaza (GAH-zah) and Tyre (TIE-er) would be destroyed because they sold God's people

into slavery. The land of Edom (EE-dum) would be destroyed because the people there wanted to get back at their own relatives in Israel for something that had happened years and years ago. People from Ammon (AM-un) would be destroyed because they murdered helpless women and children. The king of Moab (MOH-ab) and his people would be destroyed because they dug up a dead king's body and burned his bones until nothing was left but ashes!

God's people in Judah and Israel would also be punished. The people of Judah didn't follow God's laws, so He would tear down the city of Jerusalem. Israel would be punished because the Israelites stole from the poor, worshipped false gods, and lived only for pleasure.

God told Amos, "Go to the city of Bethel in Israel and tell them what I've said!"

So Amos left his flock of sheep in Judah and walked about 20 miles north to Bethel. The Israelites did not like what Amos had to say. But Amos kept telling them the truth anyway. "Seek God so that you may live! Hate evil, love good, and make justice rule in your city."

The Israelites refused to listen! They thought their mighty army, their money, their fine houses, and their pagan gods would keep them safe.

God showed Amos a vision of locusts chewing up all the plants in the fields. "Oh, Lord!" Amos pleaded. "Don't let this happen. Israel is too small." God changed His mind. He showed Amos fire burning the whole country. "Oh, Lord!" Amos pleaded again. "Israel is too small. No one will be able to go on living." God changed His mind and showed Amos a plumb line, a tool that hangs straight down to make sure a wall being built is straight and won't tumble. God said a plumb line is like His Law. Did the people of Israel measure up? Did they stand straight beside it? No! Judgment would come, and the people of Israel would become slaves in another land.

Amos told the people what he had seen, but the priest of Bethel said, "Be quiet and go home!"

Then God showed Amos a basket of ripe fruit. He said Israel was ripe for punishment for their sins. Because they had told Amos to be quiet, God said no one would be around to teach the Word of God. "The people will wander from sea to sea, seeking the Word of the Lord, but they will not find it." Amos saw still another vision. This time God was standing beside the altar, giving orders to strike Israel.

And the Assyrians (uh-SEER-ee-uns) came. Just as God had said, they destroyed Israel's army, tore down their cities, took everything they owned, and made the people into slaves.

Scripture: The book of Amos

growing time

Interesting Facts

- Many amazing things happened in Bethel. It was one of the first places where Abram (Abraham) built an altar to worship God after he moved to Canaan, the land where God had led him. It was also the place where Jacob saw angels going up and down a ladder to heaven.

- The Israelites were so wicked they couldn't wait to cheat helpless people. They had trick scales so people got less food than they paid for. They even sold as food the part of the grain that should have been thrown away. And they sold people as slaves for a pair of shoes!

Truths from God's Word

In the time of the Old Testament, God sent prophets to warn people to turn from their sin and return to Him. When people didn't listen, God punished them. (The New Testament tells how Jesus died on the cross to take the punishment for our sins. Now everyone can go to Him to be forgiven.)

Thinking about Amos

God called Amos to be His prophet. Amos had to tell about the bad things that were going to happen to people. He had to go and talk to people in a city where everyone was a stranger to him. He had to tell them that God was going to punish them. What visions did God show Amos, and what did they mean? How do you think Amos felt about his job?

Thinking about YOUR Life

There are many laws and rules to follow. We have rules at home and at school. Cities and countries have laws. And, of course, God gave us rules in the Bible. Have you ever had to tell someone that they were breaking rules? Did they change their ways? How do you act when someone tells you that you're not obeying the rules? Why is it important to obey God's rules?

Praying for Help to Obey

1. Pray that you will speak the truth about obeying God's rules, even when it seems like no one is listening.

2. Ask God to send someone to talk to you whenever you need to change your actions or attitude.

3. Pray that God will help you remember to ask Jesus for forgiveness when you disobey God's rules.

NEW TESTAMENT

Elizabeth

Elizabeth almost cried when her husband, Zechariah (zeh-kuh-RYE-uh), hugged her and said, "I will only be gone a month."

"I know." She touched his cheek. "And it is a great honor for you to be a priest. I am glad you can serve the Lord." She watched him walk down the road toward Jerusalem, where he would worship God in the Most Holy Place inside the Temple. Elizabeth knew she would be lonely without her husband, especially since they had no children.

Elizabeth had many chores to do. The servants would be getting out of

bed soon, and she would have to tell them what needed to be done. First, she would make sure they had plenty to eat for the day. After that, there was the wool to clean and make into yarn. Before Zechariah returned home, she wanted to finish the fine linen robe she had been making for him.

Elizabeth kept busy working far into the night, weaving belts and sashes on her loom. A merchant would buy them from her to sell in Jerusalem. She wanted to be a good helper to her

husband. Zechariah always said she was more precious to him than rubies!

She only felt sad about one prayer that God had not seemed to answer. She and Zechariah had prayed for years to have a child, but now she was too old to have one. How they both would have loved to have a child scampering around the house and growing up to praise God.

After a month went by, a servant hurried to the house with exciting news. "Master Zechariah is coming home!"

Elizabeth left her loom and ran down the road to greet him. When he didn't speak, she felt afraid. "What's wrong, Zechariah?" She watched as he pointed to his lips and shook his head. "You can't speak? But why?" Face flushed, eyes bright with excitement, Zechariah tried to use his hands to explain.

"An angel talked to you inside the Temple?" Elizabeth asked in amazement. Zechariah nodded and pretended to rock a baby. "The angel said I would have a child?"

Elizabeth cupped Zechariah's face. He nodded and pulled her close. They laughed and cried. Even though she was too old to have children, God was about to make the impossible possible!

That night Elizabeth and Zechariah slept together, and a baby began to form inside Elizabeth's body. Zechariah wrote that an angel of the Lord had told him the baby would be a boy and they were to name him John. He would be a Nazirite (NAZ-er-right), who would spend his life serving God. He would never eat or drink anything made from grapes—no wine or grape juice, no grapes or raisins. And he would never cut his hair or his beard. John would grow up and give the Israelites a message from God. He would tell them to get ready because Jesus the Messiah was coming!

When Elizabeth was six months pregnant, a servant told her, "Your cousin Mary has come from Nazareth, my lady."

Elizabeth hurried to the courtyard. "Mary!"

Mary looked at Elizabeth's large body and knew a baby was inside. She cried out happily, "It is true!"

At that very moment, Elizabeth felt her baby leap joyfully inside her! Because he was filled with the Holy Spirit, John knew even before he was born that God's Son, who was not yet born either, was inside Mary's body. Elizabeth looked at her teenage cousin in wonder. Mary was not married yet. But God, by the power of the Holy Spirit, had chosen to place His Son,

Jesus, inside her, so that she would become the mother of His Son. "Blessed are you among women, Mary, and blessed is your child, who is not yet born!"

Mary sang. "My soul gives praise to the Lord, and my spirit rejoices in God my Savior!"

Mary stayed with Elizabeth for three months. During that time they talked about raising their miracle babies. "The Lord will lead us every step of the way, Mary."

Soon after Mary went home to Nazareth, Elizabeth gave birth to John. On the eighth day, as was the custom, family and friends came together to celebrate. Zechariah and Elizabeth named their baby and offered him to God. The people thought the baby would be named after his father, Zechariah. But Elizabeth said, "The baby will be called John." Zechariah, who still could not speak, wrote, "His name is John." As soon as the words were written, Zechariah received his voice back. The first thing he did was to praise God!

Elizabeth and Zechariah's son grew up and went to live in the wilderness. He became known as John the Baptist. Many people went out to see and hear him. John told the people to be sorry for their sins so they would be ready to meet the Lord Jesus, the Savior of the world. When Jesus came to the Jordan River to let John baptize Him, John knew he was not good enough to do that. But Jesus said, "God wants you to do this. And it's important to do everything that is right."

Scriptures: Matthew 3:1-2, 13-15; Luke 1:5-80

growing time

Interesting Facts

- Zechariah was one of many priests. Usually each priest was able to go into the special Holy Place at the Temple in Jerusalem only once during his life. Some never got a turn.

- In the Holy Place was the Ark of the Covenant. The Ark was a wooden box that was covered with gold. Inside it were the stones on which God had written the Ten Commandments for Moses more than 1,000 years earlier!

- The priest took into the Holy Place some blood from an animal that had been sacrificed. He gave the blood as an offering to take away everyone's sins. This no longer has to be done, because Jesus died on the cross as a sacrifice for all of us.

Truths from God's Word

Sometimes it may seem impossible for God to make the things happen that He has planned for us. But we can trust Him to work out His plans at just the right time.

Thinking about Elizabeth

Zechariah didn't believe God could do the impossible, but Elizabeth did. She believed God even though she wasn't in the Temple to see the angel and hear him speak. She believed that God could give her a son even though she was too old to have children. How do you think Elizabeth felt during all the years of waiting for a child? How do you think she felt when she was told she would have a baby who would be very special? God had a plan not only for Elizabeth but also for her son, John, even before he began to grow inside her!

Thinking about YOUR Life

God knew you before you were born, and He has a plan for you, too. What are some things in your life that you feel are impossible for anyone to make happen? Is anything impossible for God? Think about the good things that can come from waiting. What do you think the Lord might want you to do today? What about tomorrow? And when you're grown up?

Praying for God's Timing

1. Pray that God will help you wait for the things He has planned for you.

2. Pray that you will always trust God to take care of you—even when it seems impossible!

3. Ask God to show you the plans He has for you each day.

Samaritan Woman

The woman needed water, but she peered out her window to make sure the other women had returned from the well. Late in the morning, when the others had gone back inside their houses, she picked up her jug and headed for the city well.

Everyone in town looked down on her. She had been married five times. Now she was living with a man who would not marry her. She felt trapped. Sometimes she dreamed of starting over, but where could she go?

She always went to the well when it was hot so the other women wouldn't be there to stare, whisper, or worse—call her names. Covering her face, she walked quickly toward the well.

She stopped when she came close, for a man sat by the well.
She could tell by His clothing that He was Jewish. Why would
He be in Samaria? Jewish people hated Samaritans. Lowering
her eyes, she approached the well.

"Please," the man said. "Give Me a drink."

She stared at Him, amazed. "You are a Jewish man, and I am
a Samaritan woman. Why are You asking me for a drink?"

The man smiled. "If you only knew the gift God has for you and who I am, you would ask Me, and I would give you living water."

No one had spoken so kindly to her in years. She felt close to tears as she drew water for Him. What did He mean by living water? "Sir, You don't have a rope or a bucket, and this is a deep well. Where would You get living water?" She lifted her chin and tried to feel important. "Besides, are You greater than our ancestor Jacob, who dug this well for us? How can You offer better water than this?"

The kind man answered, "People soon become thirsty again after drinking this water. But the water I give them takes away all thirst. It becomes like a spring inside them, giving them life that will last forever."

Oh, she knew thirst, both the kind that made her mouth and throat dry and the kind that made her soul ache inside. The ache inside was a thirst for . . . what? Forgiveness? Healing? Was there a special kind of water that would take away her sorrow and shame and make her feel like a new person? "Please, sir," she said. "Give me some of that water." She blinked away tears. "Then I'll never thirst again or have to come here to haul water and face unfriendly people."

"Go and get your husband."

The Samaritan woman bowed her head. "I don't have a husband."

"You're right," the man said quietly. "You have had five

husbands, but you aren't even married to the man you're living with now."

How could He know all that about her? And knowing everything about her, He had still spoken to her!

But she didn't want to talk about her life. Better to talk of other things. "Sir, You must be a prophet. So tell me, why is it that you Jews say that Jerusalem is the only place of worship? We Samaritans worship here at Mount Gerizim (GAIR-uh-zeem), where our ancestors worshipped." Now that she had reminded Him of the big difference between their people, the woman was sure He would stop speaking to her. But He didn't.

"Believe me. The time is coming when it will no longer matter whether you worship God the Father here or in Jerusalem."

Who was this man who spoke with such authority and behaved unlike anyone she had ever known? He went on: "You Samaritans know so little about the One you worship, while we Jews know all about Him. But true worshippers must worship the Father not only on the outside, with their bodies—their hands and voices. They must also worship deep inside with their spirits—their hearts and thoughts. They must worship the true God. The Father is looking for anyone who will worship Him that way. For God is Spirit, so those who worship Him must worship in spirit and in truth."

Would God really want her to worship Him, even after all the bad choices she had made? "I know the Messiah will come. He will explain everything to us."

"I am the Messiah."

She raised her head and looked at Him. He looked back at her, His eyes filled with love, as if she were a daughter He had been searching for and found. That look filled her with hope and joy again.

Some of the kind man's friends came toward Him and called Him Jesus. She left her jug and ran back into town. She called out to everyone, "Come and meet a man who told me everything I ever did! Can this be the Messiah, who has come to save us? Come hear what He has to say!"

The people did come, wanting to see Jesus for themselves. Then they began to drink in the words He said to them. They begged Him to stay in their town, so He stayed for two days, teaching them how to worship God.

After Jesus left, the Samaritan woman was afraid her neighbors would treat her as they had before. But many of them told her, "Now we believe Jesus is the Messiah, because we have heard Him ourselves. Jesus is indeed the Savior of the world." Then they made a circle around her and helped her feel welcome among them again.

Scripture: John 4:3-42

growing time

Interesting Facts

- Without water, neither plants, animals, nor people would be able to live. Your body is 60 to 70 percent water. It's water that helps you digest your food and keeps your body working properly. You need eight glasses of water every day, and even more when you exercise. (You can sweat out more than a quart of water during a one-hour workout!)

- Samaritans knew about only the first five books of the Bible. Because their customs and beliefs were different, Jews would not associate with them. Jesus showed how wrong their prejudice was by talking to the Samaritan woman and teaching her and her neighbors about God.

Truths from God's Word

God knows what we are thinking and feeling in our hearts. When we have made wrong choices and ask God for forgiveness, He forgives us. The living water that Jesus spoke of was eternal life. If we accept Jesus' forgiveness and love Him, we will live with Him in heaven forever.

Thinking about the Samaritan Woman

The Samaritan woman knew that she had made many wrong choices. Why do you think she didn't change her life? When she met Jesus, He knew all about her. She thought He was going to treat her badly, as everyone else had. Why did Jesus treat her so well? How do you think He made her feel? After Jesus left, what were some things the woman and her neighbors may have done differently?

Thinking about YOUR Life

All of us do things that are wrong. Other people may start treating us badly because of what we've done. Has that ever happened to you? Sometimes we have a hard time forgiving ourselves. How can Jesus help you if you need to forgive yourself and let God forgive you? Think about a time when you prayed for forgiveness and it helped you not to feel bad anymore.

Praying about Forgiveness

1. Pray that God will help you ask Him for forgiveness when you do things that are wrong.

2. Ask God to forgive you right now for something you know you should not have done.

3. Ask God to help you forgive yourself for a wrong choice you made, so that you will not keep feeling ashamed after you have been forgiven.

Lazarus (LAZ-er-us)

Martha was worried. "Lazarus isn't getting any better, Mary. We must send for Jesus!"

"Yes! Jesus is our friend. He's visited us many times. Of course He will come and help us! But where is He?"

"I heard Jesus is on the other side of the Jordan River. It takes only about a day to walk there."

So Martha and Mary sent a message. "Lord, your good friend is very sick."

But when the messenger returned, he came alone.

"Where is Jesus?" Martha wanted to know.

"I heard Him say the sickness your brother suffers will not end in death. The reason he is sick is so that God will receive glory. Everyone will praise God when they see how great and powerful the Son of God is."

The next day, Lazarus died!

Martha and Mary wept. They couldn't understand why Jesus had not come. Now all their hopes for Lazarus's healing were gone. They wrapped their brother in grave clothes and put him in his tomb. Many friends came to cry and mourn with them.

After four days, Martha overheard a servant say Jesus had arrived. *Too late,* Martha thought, *but Jesus must have had a good reason.* Without telling her sister, Martha ran out to meet Jesus. She wanted to ask why He hadn't come when they needed Him.

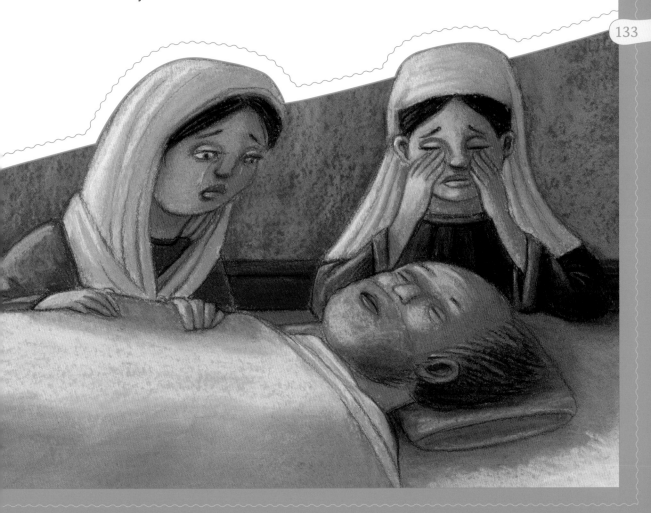

"Lord, if You had been here, my brother would not have died! Even now I know that whatever You ask of God, He will give You."

"Your brother will live again," Jesus explained.

"Yes, I know he will someday, at the end of time," Martha said, a little smile appearing on her face.

"I am the resurrection and the life," Jesus told her. "Anyone who believes in Me shall live even if he dies, and everyone who lives and believes in Me shall never die."

Martha believed every word Jesus said. She knew He was the Son of God who had come to earth to save sinners—to be their Redeemer from sin. She had known for a long time that Jesus was the long-awaited Messiah!

She ran and told Mary that Jesus had arrived. So Mary went out to Him and fell to her knees in front of Him. Crying, she said the same thing Martha had. "If You had been here, my brother would not have died."

Deeply troubled, Jesus asked, "Where have you laid him?" Mary, Martha, and their friends took Jesus to Lazarus's tomb.

Jesus wept. "Remove the stone!" He said.

"But he's been dead four days!" Martha reminded Him. "His body will smell terrible!"

Jesus spoke. "Did I not say that if you believe, you will see the glory of God?"

What could Jesus mean? Martha didn't know, but she trusted Him and ordered the stone rolled away.

"LAZARUS!" Jesus cried out with a loud voice. "COME FORTH!"

And Lazarus came back to life! Still bound tightly in his grave wrappings, he hopped out of his tomb at the sound of Jesus' voice! "Remove his grave clothes and let him go," Jesus said. So Martha and Mary rushed to help their brother. They laughed and wept for joy, finally understanding that this was how Jesus had planned all along to show the glory and greatness of God.

Lazarus had been dead, and God's Son, Jesus, brought him back to life!

Scriptures: John 11:1-44

growing time

Interesting Facts

- John 11:35 is the shortest Bible verse. You can find it in your Bible and memorize it.

- After Jewish people died, they were wrapped up in strips of cloth like a mummy.

- Jewish people were buried with a lot of spices made from sweet-smelling wood that had been ground into powder. After Jesus died on the cross, Nicodemus helped to bury Him with 75 pounds of spices mixed with myrrh, which comes from tree sap and is sticky.

Truths from God's Word

Only God has the power to bring a dead person back to life. Jesus raised Lazarus from the dead to show the people that He is indeed God.

Thinking about Lazarus

Lazarus was in the grave for four days before Jesus got to him. Along with raising Lazarus from the dead, Jesus healed his body from the rot that had already started. Do you think Lazarus was glad to be alive again? What if he had already gone into heaven? Do you think he had mixed feelings about coming back to earth after being in heaven? How do you think Lazarus's sisters felt before he died? After he died? After Jesus brought him back to life? Why do you think Jesus cried?

Thinking about YOUR Life

Have you (or someone you know) ever been so sick that you could have died? How were you healed? What did your doctor do? What did Jesus do? Do you know anyone who did die after being very sick? Will that person live again someday? How do you know?

Praying about Life and Death

1. Thank God for helping doctors know what to do when you are sick.

2. Ask for patience to wait for God's answers when you or someone you care about needs to be healed.

3. Ask God to help you trust Him to give the doctors wisdom as they treat you and other family members.

4. Thank God for the promise that all of us who believe in His Son, Jesus, will live with Him forever after we die.

Zacchaeus (zak-KEE-us)

"Jesus is coming to town!" Everyone in Jericho came out to see the young prophet who could do wonderful miracles that no one else could do. People lined both sides of the road. Zacchaeus wanted to see Jesus too, but he was so short he couldn't see over the others. And the people would not make room for him.

"Let me through!" he cried out. "Let me see Jesus!"

People moved closer together, making a wall in front of him. Zacchaeus knew they hated him. They were his own people, but he collected taxes from them for the Romans. And he always charged extra money so he could keep some for himself.

Jesus was about to pass by! Afraid that he would miss Him, Zacchaeus ran ahead and climbed up a sycamore tree.

"Look at Zacchaeus up there!" The people laughed and made fun of him.

Zacchaeus felt ashamed, but what else could he do? He had to see Jesus and hear what He had to say!

Jesus stopped when He came near the tree. Zacchaeus blushed when Jesus looked up and saw him perched on a limb.

Would the prophet make fun of him too? Would Jesus tell him he deserved to be on the outside of the group, hated by everyone?

"Zacchaeus," Jesus called up to him. "Hurry and come down, for today I must stay at your house."

The people grumbled. "Jesus will go to the house of a sinner?"

Amazed and grateful, Zacchaeus happily scrambled down. He led Jesus to his fine home and ordered his servants to prepare a feast. As Jesus spoke, Zacchaeus listened. His heart changed. He looked around at all he owned and knew that what other people said about him was true.

"I am a sinner!" Zacchaeus told Jesus. He didn't want to sin anymore. He wanted to live for God! But would Jesus believe him? Would the people?

Zacchaeus got up and opened the doors wide so the people from his town could hear. "I will give half of all I own to the poor. And if I have taken more tax money than I should have from anyone, I will give back four times as much."

The people who heard this were astonished and praised God.

Jesus smiled. "Today, salvation has come to this home. I have come to save people like you who have been lost."

God forgave Zacchaeus for his sins and welcomed him into His family as His child.

Scripture: Luke 19:1-10

growing time

Interesting Facts

- Roman law said that tax collectors could take as much money from their fellow Jews as they wanted, as long as they gave Rome the required tax. The tax collectors became rich but certainly not popular in their own country.

- God's law said that someone caught stealing had to pay back at least four times the amount he took (see Exodus 22:1). When Zacchaeus agreed to do that, he was admitting that he had taken so much tax money from people, it was like stealing.

142

Truths from God's Word

When we have wronged others, God wants us to be truly sorry about it and tell them. But that isn't enough. He wants us to show them we are sorry too. We show them by changing the way we act and making up for what we've done wrong. God also expects us to forgive others who have wronged us.

Thinking about Zacchaeus

Zacchaeus showed his changed heart by his actions—repaying more than required to the people he had stolen from. Not only did he agree to give back four times the amount he had stolen, he also said he would give half of all he had to the poor. Do you think Zacchaeus was truly sorry for what he had done? Why or why not? If so, what made him feel sorry? How do you suppose his actions changed after that day?

Thinking about YOUR Life

When you've wronged a person, sometimes it's hard to say, "Sorry." But you need to say it anyway. Do you need to make things right with anyone? How can you do that? How would you feel if you tried to make up with someone who wouldn't accept your apology? Do you believe people when they just say they are sorry? What do you think it would take for you to forgive someone who wronged you?

Praying about Being Sorry

1. Ask Jesus to help you know in your heart when you have wronged someone and to help you feel truly sorry about it.

2. Pray that you will find ways to show people you have hurt that you are sorry.

3. When people who have wronged you show they are sorry, ask for help to forgive them.

Judas

"How wonderful for you to be able to travel with Jesus! You are so blessed to be one of His disciples. Here! I hope this money will help buy what you need." A woman handed Judas a small silver denarius. Judas Iscariot (is-CARE-ee-ut) smiled and took it. Inside of himself, he sneered. The woman wore fine clothes. She could have given more! A man came next and gave a gold shekel. Much better! Judas lifted the money box just enough to see how heavy it was and then snuck a few coins into his pouch. Jesus and the other disciples would never miss them.

Jesus came toward him, a trail of poor people following behind. "Give them what we have, Judas."

Judas grew angry. "But, Lord, we hardly have enough money to buy food for ourselves and pay for a place to stay."

"Have faith, My friend. These people need the money more than we do."

He wasn't happy to do it, but Judas opened the money box and handed a coin to each person who came forward. Soon there was nothing left. Judas was glad he had already stolen some of the money for himself. He was not going to give his money away to anyone, not even Jesus!

For three years, Judas had traveled with Him, and still Jesus didn't proclaim Himself to be King of Israel. Judas grew tired of waiting! He was tired of hearing the sick, the poor, and the sad people beg for help. He expected Jesus to give His followers power to overthrow the Roman government leaders. But all Jesus did was feed people, heal them, comfort them, and talk, talk, talk! Judas wanted more from life than the few coins in his pouch.

When they reached Jerusalem, it was time for the Passover holiday, when Jews remembered how Moses had led their people out of Egypt long ago. Judas scurried away to the priests. He knew they hated Jesus for being more popular than they were. If he told them where to find Jesus, they would have Jesus arrested, and He would have to show His great power. He would have to make Himself the King or die!

"Jesus will be in the garden of Gethsemane (geth-SEM-uh-nee). I'll take you there tonight."

"How will we know which one is Jesus?"

"I'll kiss Him on the cheek," Judas said.

The priests paid Judas 30 pieces of silver. Judas was furious! Jesus was worth a hundred times more than that! Still, he took the money and left.

When Judas went to the Passover meal with the other disciples that evening, Jesus gave him the place of honor. Jesus spoke tenderly to him. He even broke off a piece of bread and gave it to him. Judas was proud. "What you are going to do," Jesus said, "do quickly." Surely Jesus meant He would make use of the opportunity Judas was giving Him to become King! All the disciples had been hoping and praying for this day. Grinning, Judas left the upper room.

But Jesus did not do what Judas expected. Instead, Jesus allowed Himself to be arrested in the garden after Judas kissed Him and the soldiers came. Jesus allowed Himself to be beaten, made fun of, and put on a cross to die between two thieves. The worst part of all was that everyone knew Judas had betrayed Jesus. Judas had double-crossed his friend and teacher, helping to murder a man who had done nothing wrong. Judas was filled with shame and wished he had never done it.

He tried to give the money back to the priests, but they said it was blood money and would not take it. Angry, Judas threw the 30 pieces of silver into the Temple. Weeping, he ran away and hanged himself.

Scriptures: Matthew 26:14-25, 47-50; 27:1-10; Mark 14:10-21, 43-46; Luke 22:1-23, 47-48; John 12:4-6; 13:2, 21-30; 18:2-3

growing time

Interesting Facts

- The amount of money Judas was given for betraying Jesus might be worth a few thousand dollars today. At that time it was equal to about a four-month salary.

- The name *Judas* means "praised and admired." Do you think anyone admires Judas now?

Truths from God's Word

Trying to do things on our own instead of God's way can get us in big trouble. As Jesus' followers, we have a choice to make. The choice God wants us to make is to listen and learn from His Son, to trust Him, and to obey His teachings.

Thinking about Judas

The disciples always had enough food and a place to stay. Why would Judas steal money that had been given for God's work? How might life have been different for Judas if he had truly loved and obeyed Jesus? When Judas understood that he had made it possible for soldiers to arrest Jesus and put Him on a cross to die, he went back to the priests. Why do you think he tried to give the money back to them? Do you think it helped? Judas never saw Jesus' resurrection or knew that he could have gone to Jesus and asked for forgiveness. How might things have been different for Judas if he had done that?

Thinking about YOUR Life

Looking at the world around us, it's easy to become greedy. We can always find something that we want more than what we already have. Have you ever stolen anything? Did you return the item and ask for forgiveness from God and the person from whom you stole it? We all disobey God sometimes. It's called sin. But everyone can ask God for forgiveness. That is the right way to live. Because Jesus died on the cross for our sins, God forgives us when we put our trust in His Son.

Praying for Forgiveness

1. Pray that you will want to do what pleases God.

2. When you do something that's wrong, pray for strength to ask for forgiveness right away so you'll have a clear conscience.

3. Ask God to help you learn from your sins so you won't repeat them.

4. Pray that you will be content with what God has given you and not be greedy.

Pilate scowled at Jesus, whom the Jewish priests brought to him. He had sent them all to Herod, hoping that the Jewish ruler would decide what to do with Jesus. Here they were back again, after Herod had made fun of Jesus and dressed Him in a purple robe.

Pilate, the Roman governor of Judea, knew what the Jewish priests wanted: They wanted Jesus killed. However, Roman law would not let them do it themselves. So they wanted him to do it for them.

One priest after another spoke against Jesus. "He claims to be a king. He tells the people not to pay taxes! He tells the people to fight against Rome!"

Pilate had heard other reports from the Jewish people: Jesus performed miracles; He healed the sick; He gave sight to the blind. The people loved Jesus, but they didn't love the priests. So Pilate understood how the priests felt. They were jealous because the people were like sheep, following Jesus instead of them.

"Are You King of the Jews?" Pilate thought Jesus would say He was not. Surely Jesus would defend Himself.

Jesus lifted His head enough to look into Pilate's eyes. "What you say is true."

Surprised, Pilate stared at Him. "So You are a king?"

"I am a King. That is why I was born. I came into the world to tell the truth."

A messenger came to Pilate with a note from his wife. "Have nothing to do with this innocent man. Last night I had a terrible nightmare because of Him."

"I find no guilt in Him," Pilate said. "Should I release Him?" He would let the people decide.

But the people had become an angry mob, and they told Pilate to release a criminal instead. The man was a murderer named Barabbas (buh-REH-bus). When they saw Jesus they shouted, "Put Him on a cross. Crucify Him!" Jesus had not come to send their enemies out of their country. He had come to talk of peace with God, and they wanted none of it!

Jesus stood silent before the angry crowd. Pilate tried to get Him to say something to save Himself. "Don't You know I have the authority to release You or have You killed?"

The priests and the people shouted, "If you release Jesus, you are no friend of the Roman emperor, Caesar!"

Pilate, the Roman governor, was afraid. How he hated these Jews! He even hated Jesus, because He was the center of the trouble Pilate was facing. He ordered that Jesus be whipped. Perhaps that would make Him speak for Himself. And if not, maybe the people would pity Him after He had been beaten.

The soldiers beat Jesus and put a crown of sharp thorns on His head. But the people felt no pity. The people kept screaming for Jesus to die. Pilate was afraid that the priests might tell lies to Caesar and get him killed. He was afraid that the people might start a riot if he did not give them what they wanted. The whole mess was out of his control.

Angry, Pilate pointed to Jesus. "Look at your King!" Then he told the guards to take Jesus away to be crucified. He also gave orders to have a sign put on the top of the cross: "Jesus the Nazarene (NAZ-uh-reen), the King of the Jews." He wanted the Jews to be ashamed of Jesus, for Pilate still thought He was just pretending to be a King.

Scriptures: Matthew 27:11-26; Mark 15:1-15; Luke 23:1-25; John 19:1-20

growing time

Interesting Facts

- Purple is the color of royalty, worn by kings. Herod's soldiers put a purple robe on Jesus to make fun of Him. They did not know that Jesus really is a King. He is King over all other kings!

- Pilate was sent from Rome to Judea to "keep the peace." Every year he let the Jewish people choose a prisoner to set free. He thought he was doing his job when he gave the people what they wanted by setting Barabbas free.

Truths from God's Word

Sometimes we have to make difficult choices. God does not force us to do the right things. It is up to us to do what we know is right, even if it means our lives will be harder because of it. But sometimes people make bad choices and do wrong things.

Thinking about Pilate

Pilate had a very hard choice to make. He knew that Jesus was innocent—He had done nothing wrong—but the people wanted Him to die. Pilate sent Jesus to die to make the people happy. Pilate was warned by his wife not to harm Jesus, but he did not listen. How did this Roman governor go about making his important decision? Did he make a good decision or a bad decision? Could God have stopped Pilate? Why do you think God let Pilate send Jesus away to die on a cross?

Thinking about YOUR Life

Perhaps someone in your class or neighborhood told you to do something you knew was wrong. If so, what did you do? Have you ever had to disagree with your friends to protect someone? What did you do? If anything like that happens again, what will you do?

Praying about Decisions

1. Thank God for teaching you in His Word what is right and good and true.

2. Ask God to help you be wise when you make decisions.

3. Tell God about any situation you are facing now, in which you know others would like you to make a wrong decision.

Thomas loved to listen to Jesus. He knew Jesus was the Messiah who had come to save the world. Thomas just didn't understand how Jesus would do that!

Thomas and the other disciples had been with Jesus when this message came from Jesus' friends Martha and Mary: "Your good friend Lazarus is very sick." Thomas worried when he heard the message, because he knew the sisters lived in Bethany. Their town was near the city of Jerusalem, where priests and other leaders of Israel hated Jesus and wanted to kill Him.

Thomas and the others listened but didn't understand what Jesus meant when He said, "This sickness will not end in death. The reason Lazarus is sick is so that God will receive glory. Everyone will praise God when they see how great and powerful the Son of God is." Jesus' followers were glad that for two days Jesus made no move to leave the place where they were staying, east of the Jordan River.

But after two days Jesus said, "Let us go to Bethany."

"No!" the disciples said. "The Jewish leaders nearby in Jerusalem want to stone you to death, Jesus, and You're going there again?"

"Our friend Lazarus has gone to sleep, and I must go to awaken him."

"If he is sleeping," they said, "he will get well!"

Jesus shook His head. "Lazarus is dead."

Thomas didn't know what Jesus was going to do, but if He had decided to risk being captured and killed, Thomas planned to be at His side. "Let us go too!" he told the others. "We'll die with Him!"

So they all had gone to Bethany, where Thomas heard Jesus call Lazarus to come out of his tomb. He saw Lazarus alive again!

But everything had changed quickly after that day. Their fellow disciple Judas Iscariot betrayed Jesus. The priests sent Temple guards and Roman soldiers to the garden of Gethsemane in the middle of the night to arrest Jesus. They held an illegal trial that Thursday night and decided He was guilty.

On Friday they got the Roman governor, Pilate, to say that Jesus should be put to death. Jesus allowed Himself to be beaten, spit upon, and made fun of before an angry mob. The Lord Jesus, whom Thomas loved and had followed for three years, was put on a cross to die on a hill between two thieves!

Thomas went away by himself and wept. He didn't understand how the Son of God could be murdered on a cross! Why hadn't Jesus called for angels to fight for Him? Nothing made sense to him anymore. Without Jesus, all hope was gone.

On Sunday, Mary found the disciples. She was so excited. "I've seen Jesus. He's alive!"

Thomas wished he could believe her, but he couldn't. Later that night he came to the upper room, and the other disciples cried out, "You just missed Him. Jesus was here. He really is alive! We've seen Him!"

In your dreams! Thomas thought. If only it was true!

"Unless I see and touch the place in His hands where He was nailed to the cross, and put my hand into His side where they speared Him, I will not believe."

The next week, Jesus entered the upper room again. This time Thomas was there. He stared, his heart full of hope again. Jesus held out His hands, palms up. "Touch Me, Thomas. Put your hand in My side."

But Thomas didn't need to touch Jesus. He knew and he wept, this time with joy!

"My Lord and my God!" He would never doubt the power of God again.

Scriptures: John 11:3-16, 41-44; 20:18-29

growing time

Interesting Facts

- After Jesus came back to life, which is called His *resurrection*, He could walk through locked doors and enter a room. But He wasn't a ghost, because He could eat and His friends could touch Him.

- Jesus had several younger brothers. (They were half brothers, because Jesus was *God's* Son, not Joseph's.) They didn't believe Jesus was the Son of God until He came back to life. Then His brother James became a church leader and wrote a book in the Bible that's named after him. He didn't doubt anymore!

Truths from God's Word

God is pleased with people who believe in His Son, Jesus. Sometimes we need to see before we will believe. But Jesus said that those who believe in Him without even seeing Him will be blessed with joy and peace.

Thinking about Thomas

Until Jesus died, Thomas faithfully followed Him. Then Thomas began to have doubts about what he believed. He questioned whether or not Jesus really was the Son of God. Why do you think Thomas had doubts? What might Thomas have expected Jesus to do when the soldiers came? As soon as Thomas saw Jesus alive and well, he never doubted again. Why do you think Thomas changed his mind about needing to touch Jesus' scars?

Thinking about YOUR Life

Some things are easy to believe without seeing. For example, you can't see or touch the wind, but you know it's there because you can feel it moving around you. What about Jesus? Have you ever felt like Thomas, wishing you could see and touch Jesus to believe He is real? Think about the little miracles that show Jesus is with you. What are some prayers He has answered? What gifts has He given you? How does He show His love through the people around you? God has also given you the Bible so you can learn about Jesus. Name one or two things you've learned about Him.

Praying about Doubts

1. Ask Jesus to help you learn all about Him so that any doubts you have will be taken away.

2. Pray that you will be able to see the miracles that happen around you every day.

3. Tell Jesus that you want Him to be your Lord and God.

Sapphira had never seen so much money.

She began to imagine all the things it could buy.

Ananias (an-uh-NI-us) looked unhappy. "I never thought the land would sell. I wish I'd never made that promise!"

They had told Peter and Jesus' other followers that they would sell a piece of land and give all the money to the church. Sapphira had felt proud when everyone praised her and her husband for being so kind and generous. But now, seeing the money, she regretted the promise just as her husband did.

Ananias took some of the money and gave it to his wife. "Hide this money. I'll take the

rest to Peter and tell him this is all we got for the land."

Sapphira agreed. "After all, it was our land, so it's our money. Why shouldn't we keep some for ourselves?"

"No one will know. And we are still giving a big gift to the church. No one has given this much before."

Ananias left to speak to Peter, and Sapphira looked for a place to hide the money. She hurried because she did not want Ananias to get all the praise for giving the money to Peter.

When Sapphira arrived at church, everyone looked at her. She felt so proud. Peter was waiting to speak to her. Sapphira was sure he was going to praise her for the gift and tell her in front of all these other people what a wonderful Christian she was to give so much money to the church.

"Sapphira, was the money Ananias brought to us the full amount you got for selling the land?"

Sapphira was angry. How dare he ask such a question!

"Yes, that was the price. Where is Ananias?" She looked around for her husband. "Ask him. He will tell you."

Peter looked sad. "No one asked you to sell your land or give all the money to the church. You and Ananias came up with that idea yourselves. When you made your promise to me about doing that, you were also making the promise to God. You and Ananias thought you could lie to God, but God knows the truth."

Sapphira and her husband, Ananias, both died that very day.

Scripture: Acts 5:1-10

growing time

Interesting Facts

- Sapphira means "beautiful" and comes from the word *sapphire*, which is a beautiful, shiny blue stone. Perhaps Sapphira was beautiful—like her name—on the outside. But when she lied and did not keep her promise to God, she was anything but beautiful on the inside.

- The people who were part of the church after Jesus went back to heaven all shared their things with one another so that no one was poor. They lived together in communes, which are like farms. Many families would live and work together in a commune.

Truths from God's Word

God always keeps His promises and expects us to do the same. He will always help us be strong enough to keep our promises. It's very important not to make promises—especially to God—that we do not plan to keep.

Thinking about Sapphira

Ananias and Sapphira could have lived long, happy lives, but they didn't. They were too interested in trying to make other people think they were great. They were not interested in pleasing God and keeping their promises to Him. What did Sapphira and her husband, Ananias, tell Peter they were going to do? What did they do instead? Can you think of one or more commandments that Sapphira disobeyed? Explain your answer. (See Exodus 20:1-17.)

Thinking about YOUR Life

Perhaps some people have broken promises to you. If so, how did it make you feel? Name some promises God has made to you. How many of them do you think He will keep? What are some promises that you might make to God? How do you think God feels if you break a promise to Him? Sometimes pleasing others is more important to us than keeping our promises to God. If you want to please God instead of being like Sapphira, what will you do about the promises you make?

Praying about Promises

1. Thank God for keeping His promises to you.

2. Pray that God will help you keep your promises to Him and to other people.

3. Tell God you want to please Him instead of trying to make yourself look great to other people.

Saul (Paul)

"We must get rid of these Christians now!" Saul said. "They are leading our people astray with their teachings about Jesus."

The Jewish leaders, including the Sadducees (SAD-you-sees) and Pharisees (FAIR-ih-sees) like Saul, agreed. "Over 3,000 people became believers in Jesus during our last Pentecost holiday! They must be stopped!"

"Let me go and find these Christians," Saul said. The leaders agreed. So Saul broke into houses and dragged men and women away to prison. Some ran away and spread the gospel in other cities. "Let me hunt them all down," Saul said. "If they won't take back what they have said about believing in Jesus, they must be killed!"

The leaders agreed with Saul. "Go and find the Christians.

Take these letters to Damascus and warn our people against believing in Jesus. Then seize His followers and kill them."

Saul looked forward to finding many believers in Damascus. But on the way there, he was shocked as a light from heaven flashed around him. Blinded by the bright light, he fell to the ground. "Saul," a voice said from heaven. "Saul, why are you hurting Me?"

Terrified, Saul trembled. "Who are You, Lord?"

"I am Jesus, whom you are hurting. But get up and go into Damascus, and you'll be told what you must do."

The others with Saul helped him get into the city and left him there. Saul prayed for forgiveness and waited. Three days later, a stranger named Ananias came to him. (This was not Sapphira's husband, the man named Ananias who had died.) "Brother Saul, the Lord Jesus has sent me so that you may receive your sight again and be filled with the Holy Spirit."

The moment Ananias spoke, thin pieces of skin like the scales on a fish fell from Saul's eyes, and he could see again! "Jesus is the Messiah!" Saul said. "He is the Son of God!"

Saul became known as the apostle Paul when he went out on his first missionary journey. He went from city to city, teaching about Jesus. He started churches everywhere he went. Many people believed Paul, learning to love and follow Jesus. But many others did not believe Paul. They hated him and often started riots when he spoke. Five times, he received 39 lashes with a whip! Once he was stoned and left for dead. But after Jesus' followers gathered around him, he was able to get up again. Three times, Paul was shipwrecked.

He worked hard as a tent maker in order to make a living and keep teaching. He traveled all across the Roman Empire and suffered from hunger, thirst, cold winters, and hot summers. He crossed rivers and mountains, and he faced robbers, angry Jewish leaders, and Romans who wanted to kill him. Everywhere Paul went, he lived in danger but still praised Jesus and trusted in Him.

In the end, Paul was put in prison for telling

the truth about Jesus being God's Son. Paul knew he would probably be put to death, but he looked forward to finishing his life on earth. He called his life a race. He was glad he had run his race well, but now he was ready to live with Jesus in heaven.

After the day Jesus spoke to Paul on the road to Damascus, all that mattered to Paul was telling everyone who would listen to him to believe in Jesus Christ. He is the Son of God, the Messiah, our Savior and Lord!

Scriptures: Acts 8:3; 9:1-19; 13–14; 15:36–28:31; 2 Corinthians 11:22-28; 2 Timothy 4:6-8

growing time

Interesting Facts

- Saul was also known as Paul. Saul was a Jewish name. Paul was his Roman name. Sometimes God changed people's names when they turned to Him. Other times it was when their position in life changed. Jesus' disciple Simon became Peter, the strong rock on which Jesus built His church.

- Even though Paul had to face angry crowds and difficult travel conditions, he went on three missionary trips. He traveled thousands of miles across the Roman Empire. And he wrote letters to individuals and churches he had visited. Thirteen of his letters are books in the New Testament!

Truths from God's Word

God is sad when people are unkind to His followers. But He forgives all who turn to Him, no matter what they have done. Anyone who becomes a believer can teach others about Jesus.

Thinking about Saul (Paul)

Paul spent the first half of his life hunting down Christians and sending them to prison. Because Jesus spoke to him from heaven, he spent the second half of his life as a Christian himself. How do you think Paul's life would have been different if Jesus had not spoken to him? How do you think Paul felt about the way he had treated Christians? We know that God forgave him, but other Christians were afraid of him at first. Do you think it was hard for them to forgive Paul? Why or why not?

Thinking about YOUR Life

Maybe some people are unkind to you or make fun of you because of what you believe. How does that make you feel? We all want everyone to agree with us. Have you ever hurt or made fun of someone who believed something that you didn't? Is it ever right to be mean to someone who doesn't agree with you? Asking for forgiveness from God and the person you wronged is always the right choice. So is showing love to everyone.

Praying for People Who Don't Know Jesus

1. Ask God to protect Christians everywhere so people who don't know Jesus will not treat us badly because of our beliefs.

2. Pray that you will never be mean to someone for disagreeing with you about who Jesus is.

3. Pray for opportunities to tell your friends and family members how much Jesus loves them.

Ananias (an-uh-NI-us)

Before Ananias met Saul, he heard shocking news about this man. Ananias had friends who lived more than 100 miles away in Jerusalem. Once in a while a messenger from there would bring a letter to him in Damascus. "Stephen was stoned to death," one said. "A Pharisee named Saul is dragging Christians from their homes and throwing them into prison!"

When Ananias heard that Saul was on his way to Damascus,

he became fearful, not only for himself but for all his Christian friends who lived in the city. He prayed, went out to warn his friends, and went to bed exhausted.

"Ananias!"

Ananias awakened and sat up. He knew right away that it was Jesus who was talking to him in a vision. "Yes, Lord!"

"Go to a street called Straight and find the house of Judas. Ask for Saul from Tarsus." (The man named Judas, of course, was not the disciple Judas, who had betrayed Jesus.)

"But, Lord!" Ananias said, a feeling of horror coming over him. "I have heard terrible things about Saul. He has caused great harm to many of Your followers in Jerusalem. And he has been sent here with the authority of the Jewish leaders to arrest anyone who believes in You!"

"Go, Ananias. Saul is My chosen servant. He will teach people about Me. Besides the Jewish people of Israel, he will teach people who aren't Jewish (the Gentiles) and their kings. And I will show him how much he must suffer for My name's sake."

If Saul became a Christian, it would be a great miracle indeed! Ananias went quickly to Judas's house and found Saul there. The man who had caused many believers to be hurt or killed was now blind, sitting in darkness and praying. "I did not see, Lord. I did not understand. Forgive me. . . ."

Ananias felt no more fear of Saul. Instead, he felt sorry for him. He really cared about Saul and wanted to help him. Ananias spoke gently as he laid his hands on this man who had been sent to destroy Christians. "Brother Saul, the Lord Jesus, who talked to you on the road to Damascus, has sent me to you. I have come so that you may receive your sight again and be filled with the Holy Spirit."

Ananias heard Saul take a quick breath and saw something like the scales of a fish fall from Saul's eyes. In their place, his eyes filled with tears of thankfulness. "Jesus is the Lord!" Saul said. "He is the Son of God!"

Ananias smiled. "Yes, He is. Jesus is Lord of all!"
After Saul was baptized, Ananias asked Judas to bring food.
Then Ananias, Judas, and Saul sat and ate together.

Jesus had performed another great miracle. He had
turned an enemy into a friend.

Scripture: Acts 9:1-19

growing time

Interesting Facts

- Damascus is one of the oldest cities in the world. People who study history think it may have existed as far back as 8000 BC. That would be around 10,000 years ago! Many buildings there today are thousands of years old. A stone church in the city is called St. Paul's Chapel.

- The street named Straight is the only street mentioned by name in the Bible and is still in Damascus today. While not totally straight, it does run straight through Damascus and used to be the main road through the city. Now it is a marketplace, with all sorts of shops along the way.

Truths from God's Word

God works through people who help carry out His plans. He is pleased when people trust Him and do what He asks, even if He asks them to do something they don't want to do.

Thinking about Ananias

Ananias knew that Saul had spent his life hunting people who believed in Jesus. Sometimes he had them put in prison. Other times he had them killed. How do you think Ananias felt when God asked him to go to Saul? Why do you think he went anyway? What helped Ananias understand that Saul was no longer an enemy?

Thinking about YOUR Life

There may be people in your church or neighborhood who are just starting to learn about Jesus. Maybe God wants you and your family to visit with them and show that you care about them. How and when could you do that? If they are new followers of Jesus, you may need to forgive them for the way they treated you in the past. A person who seemed like an enemy could become your friend. What might you do together?

Praying for People Who Don't Know Jesus

1. Ask God to make it clear to you and your family if there is a new follower of Jesus He would like you and your family to visit.

2. Ask God to help you plan things you and others in your church can say and do to help new believers grow to be more like Jesus.

3. Pray that you will do whatever God asks you to do without fear.

Dorcas

One day, in the city of Joppa, a woman named Dorcas died. Many people came to cry because they felt so sad.

"Why did Dorcas have to die?" a woman cried. "Dorcas was a wonderful friend! She made this robe for me."

Another woman sat rocking back and forth, wishing that Dorcas had not died. "She made a tunic for my son when I had no clothes for him."

"She made this coat to keep me warm," a man said.

"And she made clothes for my baby," another woman added.

Dorcas, who now lay dead, had at some time helped everyone who came. The room filled with the sound of weeping.

"It does not seem right that someone as kind as Dorcas should get so sick and die so young."

One man stood up. "Have any of you heard of a man named Peter?"

"No." The others shook their heads. "Who is he?"

"He was a friend of Jesus of Nazareth, the man some people say rose from the dead. Right now Peter is nearby in the town of Lydda."

"But what can Peter do?"

"I don't know, but we can ask him and see."

Two men left the house where Dorcas was lying on her bed. They hurried to find Peter, one of Jesus' special friends.

"I am not God," Peter told them. "I have no power over death. Only Jesus does. But take me to your friend Dorcas, and we will see what the Lord will do."

Peter went with the two men as they hurried back to Dorcas's home and followed them into her room. When he saw all the people, he asked them to leave.

Peter knew that Jesus had seen the many kind things Dorcas had done for the poor people, and he knew that Jesus understood how much these people loved and missed her. So Peter prayed over her dead body.

Then Peter spoke. "Get up, Dorcas."

She sat up. "Oh, my." Dorcas blinked and looked up at Peter. "Why am I in bed?"

Peter held out his hand. "You were dead, but now you are alive again."

Dorcas stood with Peter's help. Then he called her friends to come back into the room. They cried and laughed with joy when they saw her.

"She is alive! Dorcas is alive again!"

"Jesus is the Lord, the Son of God!"

Everyone hugged Dorcas and talked about how happy they were to know Jesus, who could bring the dead back to life.

Scripture: Acts 9:36-42

growing time

Interesting Facts

- Joppa is a city on the shores of the eastern Mediterranean Sea. It is the same city to which Jonah ran. It's where he boarded a ship to Tarshish (Spain) and tried to hide from God.

- A tunic is a shirt that is so long, it would go all the way down to your knees!

- Dorcas means "gazelle," which is a beautiful kind of deer that appears to float gracefully as it runs. The name *Dorcas* is the Greek version of *Tabitha*.

Truths from God's Word

Sometimes it is hard to take time to help others. However, God reminds us that when we help another person, we show that we care about that person. God's Word also teaches that when we love and help others, we show that we really love God's Son, Jesus.

Thinking about Dorcas

Dorcas was only one woman, but she was kind and helped many poor people. She did what she could do best when she made clothes for people who needed them. They loved her, so they went to someone they believed could help her: Peter, one of Jesus' disciples. Peter showed them that only the power of Jesus can bring a person back to life. Why did people love Dorcas so much? How did they know that she loved them?

Thinking about YOUR Life

What are some of the things you do best? Have you ever made a gift for someone? Have you ever taken time to help someone? Have you ever given some of your things to someone who needed them? How did the people you helped feel about you afterward? How do you know? Was God pleased? How do you know?

Praying about Ways to Help Others

1. Ask God to show you how you can help others.

2. Pray that God will help you think about others ahead of yourself.

3. Ask God to help you be willing to share your time and your abilities with others.

Priscilla (prih-SILL-ah)

"Welcome!" Priscilla said to those who had come to learn about Jesus. "Come in and make yourselves at home!" She and her husband, Aquila (uh-KWILL-ah), were tent makers who taught their guests about Jesus Christ. Anyone who wanted to hear the Good News was welcome in their home.

But times became difficult. Someone shouted, "Emperor Claudius has ordered all Jews to leave Rome!"

Aquila calmed their guests. "Obey the law. Be at peace."

"All you've worked for, your beautiful home! What will you do?"

"We're going to the city of Corinth."

Priscilla was not worried. "The Lord will provide all we need."
She laughed. "Besides, the emperor is helping Jesus! We would
have stayed here forever, but now we'll have the opportunity
to share the Good News with people in other places!"

And so they moved to Corinth. One day, a man came to
their door. "I've heard you are Christians. I am Paul."

"Paul!" Priscilla opened the door wide. "We've heard that the
Lord appeared to you on the road to Damascus! Come in and
tell us about it!"

"I'm looking for a place to live while I'm here in Corinth."

"Live with us!" Priscilla and Aquila said.

"The trouble that comes my way may fall upon you also," Paul warned.

"Let trouble come. We are your brother and sister in Christ. We'll help one another." Paul was also a tent maker. When he was not preaching at one of the synagogues, he worked with his new friends in their business. And he helped teach the many people Priscilla and Aquila invited into their home.

One day Paul told them, "The Lord has called me to the city of Ephesus."

"We will go with you!" So they all settled there.

Priscilla and Aquila continued to have a church in their new home, and Paul continued to preach. When the Lord called Paul away to another city, Priscilla and Aquila knew it was time to stay behind. Many of their friends were new Christians who had much to learn.

"Have you heard Apollos?" one asked. "He preaches about Jesus too, but he doesn't teach as you and Aquila do."

Priscilla and Aquila went to hear Apollos. He was a wonderful speaker, and a huge crowd had gathered to hear him. "He knows only part of the truth about Jesus," Aquila said. "He doesn't know about Jesus' life after John baptized Him. He doesn't know about the Holy Spirit!"

Priscilla knew that her husband was right. "Let's invite this young preacher to live with us. Then we can teach him so that he can teach others."

Apollos had heard of them and gladly agreed to be a guest in their home. While Priscilla and Aquila made tents, they taught Apollos everything they knew about Jesus. Apollos was eager to listen.

"Jesus taught many people about God, His heavenly Father. He healed many people too. Then soldiers put Him on a cross, and He died. But He came back to life! And He returned to heaven," Priscilla told Apollos.

Aquila explained, "The Holy Spirit is the helper Jesus spoke of. The Holy Spirit is the One God the Father sent to live inside us so that we can understand the Scriptures. The Holy Spirit is our teacher and counselor."

Apollos went out and taught hundreds of people what Priscilla and Aquila had taught him. Then many more believed in Jesus and thanked God for the Holy Spirit He gave them.

Scripture: Acts 18

growing time

Interesting Facts

- In Bible times, people made tents from black goats' hair and sheepskins. The skins were cleaned, then dried and stretched until they were soft. These soft skins could be hung over a wooden frame, poles, or branches to create a tent. For a large tent, several animal skins were sewn together. During the time of Abraham, many people lived in tents. During the time of Paul, people in cities lived in houses, but shepherds still lived in tents.

- When people moved in Bible times, they had to put all their belongings in a cart or on a donkey's back. They would walk or ride an animal such as a donkey or a camel. If their trip took them across water, they traveled that part of the journey in a sailboat.

Truths from God's Word

When people learn about God's Son, Jesus, and the Holy Spirit, who came after Jesus returned to heaven, God wants these people to teach others what they have learned. That's how the Good News about Jesus spreads from one place to another.

Thinking about Priscilla

Priscilla and her husband were glad to let Paul stay with them. What do you think they talked about while they worked on their tents? What might they have prayed about? What might Paul have told them about Jesus? When they moved to Ephesus, how did Priscilla and her husband help Apollos? What could have happened if they had not taught Apollos about Jesus and the Holy Spirit?

Thinking about YOUR Life

Before you can tell others about Jesus, you need to learn about Him yourself. You can learn by listening to teachers and by reading the Bible. How can you be sure you know everything you need to know about Jesus? How can you help someone else know all the important things about Jesus?

Praying about Knowing the Whole Truth

1. Pray that God will help you learn more about Jesus every day so that as you grow up, you will know everything you need to know about Him.

2. Ask God to help you be like Priscilla and think of things to say about Jesus while you are doing other things, like playing games and eating meals with family and friends.

3. Thank God for His Word and for the people who help you understand it.

Timothy

From the time Timothy was a little boy, his mother, Eunice, and his grandmother, Lois, had taught him to believe in God. His father, who was Greek, said there were many gods and they lived on Mount Olympus. Sometimes Timothy became very confused, not knowing what to believe!

When Paul of Tarsus came to Lystra (LIS-trah) on his first missionary trip, Timothy's mother and grandmother took him to hear about Jesus. Then Timothy's confusion ended.

"Father, you must believe. Jesus made the blind see and

the deaf hear! He raised a man from the dead! People put Him on a cross and killed Him for claiming to be God. But Jesus rose from the dead after three days in a tomb. He is the Lord!"

Sadly, the boy's father was stubborn. He still believed in false pagan gods.

Timothy went with his mother and grandmother

to hear Paul often. The young boy was eager to learn more. After Paul left town, Timothy kept learning more about the Scriptures from his mother and grandmother.

On Paul's second trip, he and Silas met Timothy, now a young man who loved the Lord. Many believers in Lystra, Timothy's hometown, and nearby Iconium (eye-KO-nee-um) knew him and thought well of him. But he wanted to learn more. "Please teach me all you know!" Timothy pleaded with Paul, and Paul was very pleased to become Timothy's teacher. In fact, he asked Timothy to join him and Silas as a missionary!

Timothy wanted to help spread the gospel. "Yes! Take me with you."

"I am going to preach in the Jewish synagogues, Timothy. I must prepare you to go there with me."

Timothy did not want anything to stand in the way of the Jewish people hearing about Jesus. He did everything he needed to do to get ready.

The Lord called Paul to go and make disciples in many different cities. Silas and Timothy traveled with him. Some of the people listened and believed. Others became upset and threw Paul out of their city.

After Paul had visited Ephesus (EH-fuh-sus) several times, he asked Timothy to stay and be the pastor at the church there. Timothy knew the Lord wanted him to stay behind, but he worried. "I'm not as bold as you are, Paul. And I'm younger than other leaders."

Paul placed his hand on Timothy as he blessed his young friend and encouraged him. "The Lord has planned for you to stay here and preach the gospel. Jesus is with you. He will give you the words to speak and show you the way to be a shepherd to this small flock of believers."

After Paul left, Timothy preached to the congregation. He visited the sick and helped those who were confused about what to believe. He taught the Scriptures. Some people did say he was too young to be their pastor. Timothy worried so much about wanting to be sure he was a good pastor that he was often sick to his stomach.

Paul wrote, "Remember the Lord, my son. Remember the gift God gave you. Trust in Jesus, and don't argue with people. Just obey God and teach what is true."

Timothy was glad to hear from Paul. He received another letter. This time Paul reminded him how his mother and grandmother had taught him from the Scriptures since he was a young boy. "All Scripture is from God and teaches us what is right and wrong. It helps us know how to do what God wants us to do."

So Timothy continued to study Scripture and teach those God had put in his charge. He loved the people in his church as he would a brother or sister, mother or father.

The young pastor obeyed the Scriptures he had been taught as a child and followed Jesus' teachings, which he had learned from Paul. He knew that everything he had been taught was true because he could trust those who had taught him.

Scriptures: Acts 14:5-7; 16:1-5; 1 Corinthians 4:15-17; 1 Timothy; 2 Timothy

growing time

Interesting Facts

- Timothy's father worshipped Greek gods. Some people thought that if they didn't do what the gods wanted, the gods would punish them. The people believed that the gods could do whatever they wanted, when they wanted. The gods, of course, were not real.

- The name *God* is in the Bible between 3,000 and 4,000 times. The name *Lord* is in the Bible between 6,000 and 7,000 times. And the name *Jesus* appears in the New Testament more than 1,000 times. That's more than 10,000 places to learn about the real God, who is our Creator and Savior!

Truths from God's Word

God teaches us about Himself and His Son, Jesus, through the Scriptures, also known as God's Word or the Bible. He places people in our lives to teach us what Scripture says and to show us the way to eternal life through Jesus.

Thinking about Timothy

Sometimes children have only one parent, grandparent, or friend who believes in Jesus. If it hadn't been for Timothy's mother and grandmother, he may never have learned the truth about Jesus. How do you think Timothy felt when his father wouldn't believe in Jesus? Why do you suppose Timothy was so interested in going with Paul? How did Timothy learn to help the people in his church? How did Paul encourage Timothy to keep on teaching people about Jesus?

Thinking about YOUR Life

Timothy learned as much about Jesus as he could, and then he taught others. Can you name some people who are helping you learn about Jesus? How can you live so that others know you love Jesus? Have you ever felt like you were too young to teach about Jesus? Timothy shows us that no one is too young to tell others about the love of Jesus. Not everyone will believe us, but we need to tell people anyway. What can you say to your family and friends about Jesus?

Praying to Learn More about Jesus

1. Pray that you will listen well to the adults who teach you about Jesus so you can learn to follow Him.

2. Pray that you will want to study the Scriptures as Timothy did so you can learn what God wants you to do.

3. Pray for courage to tell others about Jesus, no matter how young you are.

scripture index

New Testament

201

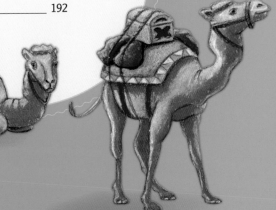

about the authors

Francine Rivers

Francine is a wife, mother, and grandmother living in northern California. She has been writing for adults for more than 30 years.

After becoming a born-again Christian in 1986, she wrote *Redeeming Love* as her statement of faith. Since then she has published numerous books and has won industry acclaim, awards, and reader loyalty. *The Last Sin Eater* won the ECPA Gold Medallion.

The characters in Francine's novels, whether real people from the Bible or fictional contemporary figures, come to life as she creates realistic conversations and background descriptions. She has written the stories of five Bible women in her Lineage of Grace series and is in the process of writing about five men in the Sons of Encouragement series. The story in each book is told from the viewpoint of one main character. And now, for the first time, Francine has used the same approach in this book of children's Bible stories.

Francine says she uses her writing to draw closer to the Lord, that through her work she might worship and praise Jesus for all He has done and is doing in her life.

Shannon Rivers Coibion

Shannon is the daughter of Francine Rivers and a full-time homemaker and homeschooling mom. She lives in northern California with her husband and two children.

Shannon, who wrote the Growing Time sections of this book, grew up in a family that read the Bible together. She was influenced not only by the after-dinner Bible readings but also by the knowledge that her parents got up early each morning to read Scripture and pray. Now Shannon lets her children know that she reads her Bible before arising each morning. And she makes certain that their schooling includes a daily reading from a one-year kids' Bible, followed by a discussion time.

about the illustrator

Pascale Constantin

Born and raised in Montreal, Pascale Constantin is the illustrator of a number of picture books, including *Camilla Chameleon*, *Raising a Little Stink*, and *Turlututu Rien Ne Va Plus*. She has been nominated four times for Canada's prestigious Governor General's Award for illustration. After spending several years in Barbados, Pascale has returned to live and work in Montreal, Canada.